PRAISE FOR *IN A BOAT IN THE MIDDLE OF A LAKE*

"Although suffering is an inevitable part of life, we value and cling to control and comfort. In this book, my friends, Patrick and Ruth Schwenk, share their personal story of being in the eye of the storm and provide practical ways to walk through difficult times while knowing that God meets us right where we are. *In a Boat in the Middle of a Lake* is a powerful reminder that our current reality is not our final reality, and God is Lord over all chaos and suffering!"

—CANDACE CAMERON BURE, ACTRESS AND *NEW YORK TIMES* BESTSELLING AUTHOR

"Patrick and Ruth Schwenk have written a book that will help you redefine personal struggles and suffering from a biblical worldview. You will not find five steps to solving your pain or hopeful platitudes. Their writing is deeply compassionate, real, and profoundly hopeful. You will read how pain, suffering, hurt, and disappointment are never without purpose, never done alone, and never hopeless in God's economy. The Schwenk's don't just know this, they have experienced it. If you find yourself in the middle of a trial, wondering *Why me?*, or wanting to encourage a sufferer, I highly recommend this book."

—DR. GARRETT HIGBEE, DIRECTOR OF PASTORAL CARE FOR THE GREAT COMMISSION COLLECTIVE, FOUNDING BOARD MEMBER OF THE BIBLICAL COUNSELING COALITION, SPEAKER, AND AUTHOR

"There are very few books these days that I can't put down, but this is one of them. For me it was a mountain and for the Schwenk's it was a lake—but for all of us, there are unexpected storms and a Savior who says, 'Peace be still.' I loved this book, its space for thoughtful reflection, its reminder that we are not alone in our suffering, and its encouragement to keep going."

—KRISTEN WELCH, AUTHOR, BLOGGER, AND FOUNDER OF *MERCY HOUSE GLOBAL*

"With the vulnerability and honesty that have long characterized their ministries of help and hope for so many families, Patrick and Ruth invite us into the boat that took them across the storm-churned waters of suffering a dreaded cancer diagnosis. They dip their feelings, fears, and faith into the lifegiving water of God's Word to remind us that Jesus is in the boat with us and has his sight set on the shore. Whatever your own journey of suffering, this is a story to remind you that no matter what the destination, Jesus will not let you drown. He will walk those waters with you all the way."

—*Clay and Sally Clarkson, founders of Whole Heart Ministries and authors of The Lifegiving Parent*

"In our broken world hardships happen, and *In a Boat in the Middle of a Lake* offers powerful reminders of how God proves over and over again how he uses hard times to push us toward intimacy, trust, and dependence on him—the only path to lasting joy and purpose. Our God is not limited to good circumstances to do something good. Thanks, Patrick and Ruth Schwenk, for writing this, and even more, for living it."

—*Michelle Myers, founder of She Works HIS Way*

"No one wants to wake up and suddenly realize they're in the center of a storm. But how many of us have found ourselves in just such a situation? And we honestly don't know where to turn or what to make of it. This is why I highly recommend Patrick and Ruth Schwenk's much-needed message shared *In a Boat in the Middle of a Lake*. These two offer powerful, compassionate, and biblical encouragement for anyone navigating those inevitably choppy waters of life."

—*Lisa Jacobson, founder of Club31Women.com*

"With a fine balance of humor and deep biblical truths, Pat and Ruth remind us that when we face suffering and hardship, God is with us. Their ability to show us how God uses pain as a catalyst to cultivate a deep, faith-filled life is something to be thankful for. We literally could not put this book down!"

—*Mike and Carlie Kercheval, authors of Consecrated Conversations: 30 Conversational Devotions for Christian Couples*

"This book was a warm balm to my soul. But it did not just comfort me—it challenged me. Pat and Ruth have walked through the valley of the shadow of death and yet remained strong through the fiercest of storms. They are honest about their wrestling with the Lord, while pointing the reader to the One who is always there for us and never fails us. If you have suffered from pain, loss, fear, or disappointment, then this book is for you—it is life-changing!"

—*Courtney Joseph, author and founder of WomenLivingWell.org*

"The phone call with a diagnosis or the sudden loss of someone you love can come like a bolt out lightening out of nowhere. Now what? Drawing on their own personal experiences, Pat and Ruth share their struggle through fear and pain. With their honesty and vulnerability, they show us that when the storms of our lives meet a good and faithful God, hope is within reach. If you are looking for a compass to help you find direction and peace in the midst of your chaos, this book is for you."

—*Sandra E. Maddox, women's ministry lead at Saddleback Church, author, and blogger at TheArtofDomesticity.com*

"Who among us hasn't received ominous news that threatened to rock our world? A medical diagnosis. A marriage in crisis. A wayward relative who is self-sabotaging. Looming financial ruin. If you feel like life's circumstances are threatening to sink you—spiritually, and maybe even physically—*In a Boat in the Middle of a Lake* is the lifeline you need. Full of personal stories and biblical encouragement, this powerful book will cause you to stop complaining, 'Lord, get me out of here!' and instead calmly ask, 'Father, why have you brought me here?' Highly recommend."

—*Karen Ehman, New York Times bestselling author of Keep It Shut, Proverbs 31 Ministries speaker, wife, and mother of three*

"*In a Boat in the Middle of a Lake* takes us on a journey—a finely woven tapestry—combining Patrick and Ruth's personal experience with key biblical texts and narratives for our understanding and growth. It is a real and raw roller coaster ride that will deepen your appreciation for the role of pain in your life and give you a new perspective as to what matters most."

—*Dave Kraft, author, speaker, and leadership coach*

"Through the pages of this book, Patrick and Ruth pastored parts of my heart that I didn't realize needed pastoring. We need voices like theirs in times of great uncertainty, and even in times of perceived security. Their words were a gift to me."

—Sara Hagerty, author of *Adore: A Simple Practice for Experiencing God in the Middle Minutes of Your Day*

"This book is a tangible gift for those sitting in their own boat wondering if Jesus cares about them. Dipping their pens in the words of 2 Corinthians 1:4, Ruth and Pat offer real comfort to fear-filled followers of Christ because they themselves have found him flawlessly faithful. I am grateful for the grace they extend in letting us 'tether' our boats to theirs and encouraging us to deeply trust that Jesus will get us to the other side just as he promised."

—Stacey Thacker, author of *Threadbare Prayer: Prayers for Hearts that Feel Hidden, Hurt, or Hopeless*

"For anyone searching for hope in a dark or desperate season, *In a Boat in the Middle of a Lake* beautifully touches on all of the ways God is working in our lives to bring hope in our suffering and transform our hearts through his amazing grace. No pain is ever wasted, and Patrick and Ruth are proof of that. I cannot say enough good things about this book. It is one I will read over and over again. It is the reminder we all need that God is good, he is for us, and he is making all things new."

—Amber Emily Smith, wife of Granger Smith, actor, philanthropist, and influencer

IN A BOAT IN THE MIDDLE OF A LAKE

TRUSTING THE GOD WHO MEETS US IN OUR STORM

Patrick and Ruth Schwenk

An Imprint of Thomas Nelson

In a Boat in the Middle of a Lake

Published in Nashville, Tennessee, by Nelson Books, an imprint of Thomas Nelson. Nelson Books and Thomas Nelson are registered trademarks of HarperCollins Christian Publishing, Inc.

Published in association with the literary agency of Brock, Inc., P.O. Box 384, Matthews, NC, 28105.

Thomas Nelson titles may be purchased in bulk for educational, business, fundraising, or sales promotional use. For information, please e-mail SpecialMarkets@ThomasNelson.com.

ISBN 978-1-4002-1688-8 (eBook)
ISBN 978-1-4002-1687-1 (TP)

Library of Congress Control Number: 2020936473

Printed in the United States of America

HB 06.28.2021

To Tyler, Bella, Noah, and Sophia:
May God, who is your perfect and forever Father,
give you grace to walk humbly with him. And in
your generation, may you be found faithful; fully
devoted to Jesus no matter what storm you face.

To our fellow companions in a boat:
May you meet Jesus in your storm and find him faithful,
good, and trustworthy. And may he be your joy,
strength, and hope until he gets you to the "other side."

CONTENTS

CHAPTER 1

IN A BOAT IN THE MIDDLE OF A LAKE

Would you spell that for me?" I (Patrick) asked the nurse over the phone. My head was already spinning. Heart pounding. I scribbled a word that I had, until now, never heard before onto the only scrap piece of paper I could find in our car. A word that would turn our world upside down.

For nearly four months, I had known something was wrong. My wife, Ruth, and I are both over forty, so we've grown accustomed to less energy, more body aches, and "injuring" our necks just from sleeping the wrong way. I've always been accused of being a bit of a hypochondriac, but this time was different. My body wasn't right. And I knew it.

The first signs were a kind of chronic and nagging bone pain, mainly in my spine and wrists. Then my body struggled to heal from an ear infection. In November of that year, I injured my left hip. A week later, I injured it a second time. The pain became so severe I had trouble walking and could not lift my left leg without assistance. By December, my muscles were growing increasingly fatigued. So much so that most Sunday mornings I would sit during my sermons.

My doctor eventually ordered an X-ray, which looked pretty normal. But, suspicious there was more going on, he referred me to an orthopedic specialist. "You shouldn't be in this much pain," he told me. I agreed. He ordered another scan, an MRI.

Christmas was just a week away. So when the doctor called to go over the results, we were hoping to have some closure. We thought peace of mind would be a nice present. But instead of getting answers, we ended up with more questions.

"We found a lesion," my doctor said. "A tumor. It's deep in your hip socket, where your hip meets your pelvic bone."

More questions.

More waiting.

More tests.

By the time the nurse called that day in January, we had been waiting for nearly a week for the results of my lab work, ordered by an oncologist from the Rogel Cancer

Center of Michigan Medicine. We had just picked up our oldest son, Tyler, and his friend from school when my cell phone rang.

The nurse spelled out an unfamiliar word. Sensing my confusion and attempting to break the silence, she finally said, "It's a type of blood cancer, and we are referring you to a specialist. I am sorry."

The word *cancer* rattled around my brain like a pinball bouncing back and forth, looking for a place to land. A place to register. And then it dropped. Sinking into my heart. Shredding everything in its path.

I was trying to figure out how to tell Ruth. I needed to tell Ruth. And yet, at the same time, I was trying not to let our son know. I was trying to breathe. Trying to recover from the punch in the gut. Except the pain didn't stop.

Water. It all felt like raging water. A furious storm. Waves crashing around us. With one word, we had been thrust into the deep. Darkness surrounded. And the shore was nowhere to be found. Or seen.

We wanted to go back to dry ground. To the shore. Even as we write this, it seems unreal. It feels like we are telling someone else's story. Not mine. Not ours. But it *is* ours. This is our life. This is our storm. It's our boat.

We are in a boat in the middle of a lake.

This is our story, and we are sure you have yours. At some point, we all find ourselves in a boat in the middle of a lake. We all find ourselves in water. In a storm. And far from shore.

For some, it is the loss of a loved one. A disability. The revelation of an unfaithful spouse. The loss of financial prosperity and security. A miscarriage. And the list goes on.

Because you are reading this book, it likely means you are in a storm too. Or maybe you're just finally reaching the shore. We should probably say up front—we're not experts on suffering. Some of you reading this have suffered worse. Your pain is more severe. Your loss greater. We don't own the corner on chaos. We're just fellow companions, limping along with you. Fighting to stay afloat. Trying to find our way. And learning to let God meet us and mold us.

That's what this book is about. It's about water and the ways God uses it and meets us in it. After all, your story and our story, it's all really his story—it is his work.

If you are anything like us, we're guessing you'd love to be back on the shore where you have your footing and it's dry. And yet, as much as we would prefer to be *by* the lake rather than *in* it, we wouldn't trade this storm and what God is doing for anything. We say that with a bit of fear and trembling. With humility. But we do mean it.

We have tasted and seen God's goodness. We feel a little like Job, who said, "My ears had heard of you but now my eyes have seen you" (Job 42:5). After all, our God is the God who meets us in our storm. And what he gives us in a boat in the middle of the lake is what he could never give us on dry ground.

January 17, 2018, transformed our lives. It was also a turning point; we began to wrestle with how God wanted us to walk through this. How do we faithfully and humbly trust him in the midst of this? What does God want to teach us? How is he drawing us to himself, desiring to deepen our faith? And with four kids—who at the time were fifteen, thirteen, eleven, and nine, we wondered, How do we model an honest faith, one marked by trust, hope, and obedience? How does God want to meet us and mold us in the water?

NEW LOCATION, NEW LESSON

Ruth and I have always had a love-hate relationship with water. This might sound odd, considering we live in Michigan, a state bordered by four of the five Great Lakes. Depending on how you count them, there are over eleven thousand lakes in Michigan. That is a lot of water.

Let's just say we prefer looking at water to being in water. It's beautiful to the eye and cold to the touch, in our opinion. Which is why, when we go kayaking, one of our favorite family activities, we have to harness ninja-like maneuvers to get from the dock to the kayak without becoming one with the water!

Complicating matters, we have four kids who love the water. Lakes and pools and oceans. All of it. They love to look at it, be in it, splash in it, and, in general, they would be content to just stay in it. Not us. Ruth wears yoga pants to the pool. I wear jeans. When we are feeling extra daring, we roll up our pant legs to mid-shin and dip our toes in the water. Slowly.

This has nothing to do with modesty and everything to do with comfort. Like we said, we prefer looking at water to being in water.

One of my most terrifying memories as a child happened at church camp. As you might expect, it had to do with water. As best as I can remember, I was around ten or eleven.

Every year church camp rolled around like a dentist appointment. I knew it was good for me, but I always dreaded it. What elementary-aged boy doesn't enjoy a week away from home in the woods? Everyone else seemed to enjoy it—it seemed like the highlight of their year. I, on the other hand, wasn't as sold, and this particular year was especially painful for me.

One afternoon, one of the camp counselors lined up all the boys along the shore. On the beach. Next to the water. *So far so good*, I thought to myself.

Then the surprise came.

The counselor announced that he would be teaching us how to tip over a canoe and then get back in it. This was not what I expected, but it was all still good. Still safe as long as this lesson remained on the beach.

For thirty minutes we listened intently. We watched him pretend he was in the middle of the lake. Wide-eyed, we attached our gaze to his canoe. And then we tried it ourselves. Pairing up, we pretended to be in the water in the middle of the lake. We tipped our canoes over, imagining what it would be like to feel the rushing water fill our canoe. And then, safely and easily, we tipped our canoes back upright.

Here is where the fear comes in. If that would have been the entire lesson, I might have gone back to church camp the following year. But our counselor had one more surprise. Like a herald announcing good news, he proclaimed we were now moving our lesson from the shore to the middle of the lake. It was not enough to know how to tip a canoe back over *by* the lake; we needed to know how to do it *in* the lake.

My memory gets fuzzy here. I'm alive, so I know I survived the lesson that day in the water. But the experience is one reason for the love-hate relationship I have with water.

As it turns out, the Bible is full of water stories and seems to have a similar love-hate relationship. Some stories of water in the Bible are good, and some are bad. But the point is that Jesus used water as an essential ingredient and environment for teaching.

One of those water stories we'll come back to over and over is found in Mark 4. Mark begins by telling us that Jesus was teaching "by the lake." He wrote, "Again Jesus began to teach by the lake. The crowd that gathered around him was so large that he got into a boat and sat in it out on the lake, while all the people were along the shore at the water's edge" (Mark 4:1).

Much like my camp counselor, Jesus had a captive audience lined up on the shore. They, too, were likely wide-eyed and listening intently. But they were safe. And dry.

Interestingly, he started by telling them a parable about a farmer and his seed. A story about land and dirt—not water (that would come). The farmer represented Jesus, who went out planting seed (God's Word). Some seed fell "along the path" (v. 4). Its soil was hard. The seed could not penetrate it, and so it died. This kind of heart is like a person who hears about God's truth and love and grace but quickly has God's Word snatched away by the Enemy.

Other seed fell on rocky soil (v. 5). It showed some signs of life, at least for a little while. But this soil was shallow. The seed had no roots, and where there are no roots, there is no fruit. When trouble comes, this person quickly turns away.

"Other seed fell among thorns" (v. 7). The worries and stresses of life and the deceitfulness of wealth choked it out. This heart is crowded. It's not a consumer heart as much as it is a consumed heart—consumed with everything but God. There is no room for Jesus in this heart.

"Still other seed fell on good soil" (v. 8), where it "produced a crop"—a hundred, sixty, or thirty times what was sown. This is the kind of heart that receives God's truth and love. It roots itself in who God is and what God desires. As a result, it is fruitful.

This is the heart Jesus is after. This is the heart he wants for us. A good heart, like good soil, that receives the seed of God's Word—that receives God himself. A person who walks with God. Knows him. Delights in him. Remains faithful. Perseveres. Serves and obeys Jesus from a place of intimacy.

But seed cannot grow on its own. New life, abundant life, has to be cultivated.

One of our favorite activities is gardening. Or maybe I (Ruth) should say that one of my favorite activities is buying plants and deciding where they should go in our landscaping. Patrick is less enthusiastic when it comes to the actual digging and planting and maintenance of it all. But one thing we both know is that planting seeds or new vegetation is pointless without water.

Water is one of the key ingredients for seed to bring forth life, to grow. Likewise, our faith needs water to grow. Of course, our faith also needs dry ground and time on the shore. If faith is to be tested and proven genuine, it eventually needs water.

After this opening parable, Jesus told several more stories about God's kingdom. Eventually he taught a lesson in the water. But the disciples didn't know what was coming. Standing by the shore that day, they didn't expect their teacher to switch locations. This is where Jesus did something surprising, much like the camp counselor. He was not content to keep giving lessons by the lake. He had to get the disciples wet. He had given them enough seed.

It was time to cultivate the soil of their hearts, where his seed, his word, could be watered and grow and produce an abundant crop. Where it could change them.

Jesus had to get the disciples away from dry ground. My guess is they were content and comfortable on the shore. But as much as comfort can be our friend, it can also be our enemy. Have you ever been just fine where you are? Your health is good. You have plenty of money in the bank. Your job is secure. All of your kids are healthy. Life makes sense. God is behaving like he should, or at least like you think he should. And then Jesus says, "Follow me. You've learned enough *by* the lake. Let's go *in* the lake."

This is exactly what Mark recorded Jesus doing with his first disciples. Jesus shifted his location as he shifted his lesson.

> That day when evening came, he said to his disciples, "Let us go over to the other side." Leaving the crowd behind, they took him along, just as he was, in the boat. There were also other boats with him. A furious squall came up, and the waves broke over the boat, so that it was nearly swamped. Jesus was in the stern, sleeping on a cushion. (Mark 4:35–38)

Just like that, the disciples found themselves in water instead of by water. It was getting dark. Evening was coming. And where there is water, there are also waves. Before long, these waves were threatening the very lives of these young followers of Jesus.

But if not for the storm, they would never discover the goodness and power and faithfulness of the God who was with them. Without fear, they would never know faith. Without hurt, they would never know hope.

It's worth noting that the Bible often uses the imagery of water to illustrate or symbolize chaos and disorder and evil. Think for a moment about the opening chapters. The writer of Genesis told us that "In the beginning God created the heavens and the earth. Now the earth was formless and empty, darkness was over the surface of the deep, and the Spirit of God was hovering over the waters" (Gen. 1:1–2).

There was water. And darkness was over the surface of the deep. But God was there too. From out of the chaos and darkness of those murky waters, God spoke. He put the chaos in its place. He showed his rule over it, subduing it by speaking to it and over it.

> Some lessons we can learn only in the midst of chaos, not in a classroom.

It's no wonder Mark records that Jesus was the only one unmoved by the storm. The chaos of the water and storm were no threat to Jesus. In fact, he was in the stern of the boat, sleeping on a cushion. At rest. This was going to be a lesson not for Jesus but for the disciples. And for us.

We need water to grow. And some lessons we can

learn only in the midst of chaos, not in a classroom. And no matter how we get there, we can trust the God who meets us in our storm.

ANOTHER PICTURE OF WATER

Here is where we want to encourage you. Water is not all bad.

On the one hand, as we have already seen, water can be a picture of chaos in the Bible. But this is not the only picture the Bible paints.

In the Gospels we see Jesus meeting Peter on the water after a long night of fishing. Peter had come up empty, with no fish to show for his hard work of casting nets. Jesus told him to try again: "Put out into deep water, and let down the nets for a catch" (Luke 5:4).

This must have been a little frustrating. After all, Peter was a fisherman. He must have thought Jesus was crazy when he told Peter to let down the nets again. Especially since he had been letting down the nets all night. What did Jesus know about catching fish?

"We've worked hard all night and haven't caught anything. But because you say so, I will" (v. 5). Probably a bit reluctantly, Peter took Jesus at his word. What was the result? Such a large catch that it nearly ripped open his nets. An illustration, for sure, of what the disciples would become: fishers of men.

But there is another lesson here. Do you see the Bible's multifaceted treatment of water? Water is not just evil and chaos. It's not just the abyss. When Peter pulled his nets full of fish into his boat, he discovered that water is also a place of great abundance.

Jesus, as God among us, is Lord over the water. He knows the deep. He knows the water. He knows our water. He didn't cause our storm. He uses the water. He is leading us in and through it. And he is with us in the middle of whatever lake we find ourselves in.

Don't miss this. Water, with all its waves, can be the place of our greatest anxiety, but it can also be the place of our greatest abundance where God begins something new. Something different and deeper in us.

Jesus is not shaken by the swirling waves we are in right now. He is Lord over the chaos. King over its contents. We are not alone in a boat in the middle of a lake. And even when Jesus doesn't stop the chaos around us, he can still the chaos in us.

Jesus is with you. And while he is not moved by the waves, he is moved by you. His heart is close to yours.

> Even when Jesus doesn't stop the chaos around us, he can still the chaos in us.

And this is why water, the storms we find ourselves in, can also be such abundant places. While we live in a culture that values strength, control, and comfort, God does his greatest work in us through our pain. He transforms us in trials. It's when we feel overpowered and overwhelmed that God has us right where he wants us.

The storms are real. Danger is often all around. But water is one of the places God chooses to meet us to grow those seeds of his truth, love, and promises, that are planted in our heads but need to take root in our hearts. The water we receive in the storms we face is often the perfect, albeit painful, ingredient God uses to grow us.

Are you in a boat in the middle of a lake? The waves can be disorienting. The storms can feel devastating. Sometimes they *are* devastating. But that storm is never where God leaves us. We might be in a place of great anxiety, but we are also in a place of great abundance.

That's what the rest of this book is about. So let's enter the waves. Let's enter the classroom of chaos. And together let's not just meet God but be transformed by him.

QUESTIONS FOR FURTHER REFLECTION AND DISCUSSION

1. Describe a time when you found yourself "in a boat in the middle of a lake."
2. What was your first reaction to your storm and why?
3. In what ways can our own comfort be an "enemy" of how God wants to shape us?

4. Why is chaos, and not a classroom, often a better teacher?
5. How has your place of anxiety also been a place of abundance?

CHAPTER 2

IT'S OKAY TO NOT BE OKAY

We know lots of ways to describe pain and loss. It often feels like a pit. It feels like a deep and dark abyss, a hole that grabs us when we hurt, where we hurt, and sucks us in. Sucks us down. It's a hole that can be hard to get out of.

The psalmist said it well and honestly: "You have put me in the lowest pit, in the darkest depths" (Ps. 88:6). Pain can feel like a hole our loss throws us in. And maybe even a pit we feel God has thrown us in.

Just today, as we were writing this chapter, we heard the heartbreaking news of a couple we know who lost the youngest of their three children in a tragic accident. We can't begin to imagine what they are feeling or what they are facing. The hole they are now in is deep. And dark. The pain must feel crushing.

We felt the pain and the feeling of being in a pit halfway through the physician assistant's explanation of the cancer Patrick was facing. We'd already heard the word *cancer* eight days earlier on the phone. Now it was time to understand it. Talk treatment options, life expectancies, and possible outcomes. It was time to face reality. A new reality. Our reality.

And we weren't quite ready to accept it all.

That's when we lost it. We had held it in long enough. The PA put her hand on mine (Patrick's) and let me cry. I grew up with two older sisters, so crying has always come easy, but this was a new kind of sadness. A darker sadness. A deeper hole. A deeper hurt.

Simply put, pain is loss. And loss hurts. I had just lost my health. And it felt like I was losing a lot more. My security. Energy. Parts of my identity. Maybe even my future. Our family. It felt like cancer was threatening everything. The loss, and potential loss, hurt. It was a pain we had never known before.

We didn't care that the PA in front of us was a stranger. We wept anyway. In pain, our hearts ache. We long. Our hearts grieve what they can't get back. It can feel suffocating.

Those early days and weeks of diagnosis were ugly and messy. We sucked it up when we had to, hiding some of our emotions for the sake of our children's security. The world didn't stop for us. Our friends, who loved us and supported us well, had lives that went on too. And ours also had to continue, to a certain degree. But it wasn't pretty. And we still cried a lot. Nearly everywhere and at the drop of a hat.

We cried on our way to the store.

We cried in the store.

We wept during worship.

I cried in nearly every sermon I preached.

In the coffee shop.

At our son's basketball game.

Alone, in the bathroom.

No place was off limits for our pain. It was impossible to hide from hurt—it followed us everywhere. There was no escape.

As we could, we met with or called friends, family, and ministry leaders. Through tears, we shared the news. We asked questions together. At times we were angry. We cried together, but we also sought God together. We prayed and worshiped. All of it was messy. And that was okay. It *is* okay. The road to healing is never a straight line. The boat ride from one side of the lake to the other is choppy, bouncy, and never perfect.

But if we are to move toward healing, we need to remember that God is okay with our hurt. He welcomes it. As it turns out, the Bible has a lot to say about learning to lament.

LAMENTING LEADS US TO GOD

The Bible is full of honest cries and questions in the midst of storms. They are called laments. We're guessing the word may not be familiar. After all, many of the songs we sing in church or listen to on the radio are much more positive, uplifting, and encouraging. Few of us sing sad songs. Yet the Bible is full of these sad songs and cries of the heart—these laments.

The word *lament* simply means to express sorrow or grief. Which is probably why most worship leaders stay away from laments—they are pretty depressing! Usually we are trying to cheer people up when they come to church, not further discourage them. But laments have a different purpose. They are for different seasons and circumstances—the hard seasons. They have their place and their purpose. Especially when we are experiencing and entering our pain.

Over a third of the book of Psalms are these honest cries of the heart. Cries of despair, confusion, fear, anger, disappointment, and depression. But also cries of hope and trust in the midst of suffering.

Any step toward healing or transformation has to start first with feeling the pain before trying to figure out the pain.

Any step toward healing or transformation has to start first with feeling the pain before trying to figure out the pain. And that is what lamenting invites us to do. Consider just a few examples:

- "I am worn out from my groaning. All night long I flood my bed with weeping and drench my couch with tears." (Ps. 6:6)
- "My God, my God, why have you forsaken me? Why are you so far from saving me, so far from my cries of anguish? My God, I cry out by day, but you do not answer, by night, but I find no rest." (Ps. 22:1–2)
- "Save me, O God, for the waters have come up to my neck. I sink in the miry depths, where there is no foothold. I have come into the deep waters; the floods engulf me. I am worn out calling for help; my throat is parched. My eyes fail, looking for my God." (Ps. 69:1–3)
- "Why did I not perish at birth, and die as I came from the womb?" (Job 3:11)
- "Why is my pain unending and my wound grievous and incurable?" (Jer. 15:18)

Do any of these strike a chord? Do any of these laments remind you of your own? Our guess is that they probably do. Their honesty is an expression of our humanity. Our shared hurt.

When we lament, we are refusing to live in denial. We are acknowledging real hurt. We are naming the pain. Putting words around a real wound. When we lament, we are admitting the world is not right. It's not as it should be. It's not what it was, and it is not yet what it will be. When we lament, we are resisting the temptation to run from God. To lament is not only to hurt but also to take our hurt to God. Our focus should never be on the hurt alone. Otherwise, we can become consumed with it instead of transformed by it.

For some people, suffering causes them to doubt God's existence. Their hurt or disappointment leads them to walk away from their faith. They give up. But where do they turn? If we are just accidents, alone in the universe, then why do the things that go terribly wrong not feel right? If we are just surviving, getting by longer and better than others, then why are we so moved by tragedy, injustice, sickness, and seemingly senseless evil? Why does cancer, miscarriage, premature death, or an unfair job termination hurt so badly?

The answer is because we know better.

Because deep down we all carry the faint memories of life as God intended in the garden of Eden (Gen. 1–2). Deep down we all know there is a God. That life and joy and beauty and truth and goodness and justice are real things. Sacred things. Things essential to what it means to be human. This is why pain proves God's existence. Something is desperately wrong from what we all know, and feel, to be true. Getting away from God is not the answer. Getting back to him is.

And for others, it's not so much that they come to

doubt God's existence; they question God's character. Perhaps these are even scarier questions to wrestle with. As we began to enter the pain and feel the weight of our situation, we couldn't help but ask these types of questions:

Is God really good?

Does he love me?

Can we trust his promises?

Is he really faithful?

If there is a God, is he wise or powerful?

All legitimate questions. God is big enough to handle all of it. He is okay with our hurt and our questions and our crying. The lamenting is meant to lead us to the heart of God.

So how do we lament? What does that even look like? For starters, we have to be honest.

BEING HONEST ABOUT THE HURT

One of the best things we can do in our hurt is be honest. We need to be honest: with ourselves, with others, and especially with God.

We need to be honest in our prayers.

Honest in our conversations.

We need to pour out our hearts in honesty when we journal.

And be honest when we worship.

We live in a culture that tends to numb the pain. Deny it. We are often tempted to distract ourselves. Entertain ourselves. And many times while walking through suffering, we even feel the pressure to have it all together for the sake of others.

But if God is going to meet us and mold us in the storm, what we need most is to be real. As much as we'd love to escape our pain, it's important to remember that we first have to enter our pain.

Entering our pain is healthy because eventually it leads to healing. While we almost always enter pain suddenly, we have to move through it slowly. We can't encourage you enough to honestly enter your pain with someone else. Maybe it's your local pastor. A qualified counselor or therapist. A spiritual guide. Or trusted friend. Whoever it is, it's helpful to keep in mind that we often move through different stages of grief.

Most people, when they find themselves in a boat in the middle of a lake, respond in shock and denial. We feel the pull toward that pit of pain. We go numb. What has happened, or is happening, seems unreal. Impossible. We resist reality. And for a season, we refuse to accept the pain.

Denial most often leads to an avalanche of emotion. We feel it all. Everything from fear to anger to sadness and sometimes guilt. When the shock wears off, the emotions set in. It can all feel like a slide to the bottom of a pit.

Many writers talk about another stage of grief: trying

to bargain. We may try to negotiate in an effort to get out of the mess we're in.

"God, if you get me out of this, I'll be more faithful to you."

"I'll be a different husband."

"A new kind of mom."

"A better father."

"If you answer my prayer, then I'll love you like I know I should."

These are different ways we might try to make a deal to cope with our pain.

We all experience these stages of grief, maybe even more than once, in our suffering. Sometimes a stage might last for months. Other times, for minutes. That's the thing with not being okay—it's messy. Not so clean or linear or straight. We never entirely graduate from one stage to the next. But there are ways that we grow *through* our grief, even if we never grow *out* of our grief.

What's important right now, what we would want you to know, is that it is okay to not be okay. It's okay to be a mess. It's okay for people to see that the process is not pretty and for others, even friends, to see and feel the weight of your hurt.

Shortly after Patrick preached a sermon on God feeling absent, a man who attended our church at the time approached us and shared the story of losing his sister. With tears in his eyes, he confessed, "I just don't know what to do or how to do it right."

That's the thing with hurt—there is no clear-cut path through the pain. We need to enter it and move through it slowly. Don't feel rushed—as if you are taking too long to get your act together. It's not okay to feel foolish for feeling fearful. Don't believe that somehow your sadness is a reflection of your lack of faith. It is okay to feel out of place and not at home. It's okay to cry, to look and feel out of sorts.

We'd love to put our arms around you, put our hands on yours, and just be with you. Listen to you. Cry with you. And encourage you with what you already know. We are sorry you're experiencing this pain. We'd remind you that God is going to give you the grace to keep going. There is grace when we need it, when we experience pain and enter our pain. One step in front of the other. One breath at a time.

If you are questioning and crying and hurting, it means you are human. It means you are honest. And that is a good place to be. After all, a healthy spirituality is an honest spirituality. We can be tempted to rush the hurt. We can almost feel ashamed of the pain, as if it means we don't have enough faith or we're not good enough Christians. We're embarrassed at our lack of trust. Surprised at how quickly our convictions shriveled into questions. Concerned that we are a burden on those who are walking through the deep waters with us. We certainly have felt that way.

During our pain we think many people just assumed

we were okay. After all, we're in ministry. A pastor and pastor's wife. We have this faith thing figured out. Until we don't, of course. For nearly twenty years, we loved and served and ministered to those "in a boat." Then we were the ones alone. Disoriented. Depleted.

Serving and giving out of that place is painful and, if not by God's grace, impossible.

And so we, too, had to be honest. With ourselves. With our friends. And with our church. We were hurting, and it was going to be a long, choppy boat ride to shore. None of it looked pretty.

But it was not permanent either.

PAINFUL BUT NOT PERMANENT

We want to remind you of one more thing. Suffering hurts. It requires our honesty. It is never pretty. But our current reality is not our final reality.

This is the theme of the Old Testament book of Lamentations, an entire book containing only laments. Somewhere around 586 BC the Babylonians showed up and destroyed Jerusalem. The temple, the Jewish people's place to meet with God, was reduced to rubble. And if that wasn't bad enough, many of the people were taken out of the land God had given them. They were living as exiles.

They, too, were hurting. They felt separated from

God, perplexed by what he was doing and what he had allowed. The book of Lamentations is their honest expression of hurt. But it's also their humble return to God.

One of the interesting facts about this short book is that God's voice is silent. Nowhere does he speak. And maybe that is part of the purpose and the point. In lament, God's silence is our space to speak. To cry out from the heart. Grief. Pain. Repentance. Faith, even if feeble. And questions. Lots of questions.

There is one thing we don't want you to miss. We want to encourage you that our deepest hurt is also where our greatest hope emerges. While we experience pain and loss, those circumstances are also the fertile soil for new beginnings. For new life. For a new day.

We will never be the same. We know you won't be either. That's the way loss works. The hurt always leaves its mark. But we also know the pain has a purpose.

We will never be the same . . . for the better.

Accepting hurt never means you are over the hurt. It means you've come to grips that this reality really is yours. It's your boat. Your lake. You're coming to terms with the fact that, with every death, there is new life.

This is one of the things that is so beautiful about this short and sad book of Lamentations. Right in the middle of the hurt and pain there is the promise of new life. Like a protest to the pain, there is this proclamation of God's goodness and the newness of life in him.

You'll notice that almost exactly in the middle of the

book, the following verses emerge. There is chaos and pain and hurt to the left. And all the same to the right. But in the middle is hope, an invitation to trust God in spite of how we feel:

> Yet this I call to mind
> and therefore I have hope:
> Because of the LORD's great love we are not
> consumed,
> for his compassions never fail.
> They are new every morning;
> great is your faithfulness.
> I say to myself, "The LORD is my portion;
> therefore I will wait for him."
> The LORD is good to those whose hope is in him,
> to the one who seeks him;
> it is good to wait quietly
> for the salvation of the LORD. (Lam. 3:21–26)

Right there in the mess is this affirmation that God is still good. He is faithful. He is loyal to his people. He will not forsake us or forget us. Our pain is not pointless or wasted. Our hope is anchored in him, and the Lord is good and has good things for us.

And maybe this is what hurt does. The depth of our hurt enables us to know the depth of hope and life forever with God. This "living hope" that is ours because Jesus is alive? It is a gift no one can take away from us.

Hope offers us new beginnings. Suffering gives us a new purpose. Storms may lead to new relationships that didn't exist before. And trials can create in us new dreams.

We know it might seem impossible to envision right now. We know there may be things we've lost that we'll never get back. But biblical hope enables us to see differently. To see our pain, feel it, but not be consumed by it. To see through it and see God's purpose for it.

Hope reminds us that our current reality is not our final reality.

Hope reminds us that our current reality is not our final reality.

"Yet this I call to mind and therefore I have hope," the writer of Lamentations said. This reality, this season, these circumstances, this hurt will not last forever. It doesn't have to last forever. God wants to give you hope. His hope.

Here's the good news. Even Jesus experienced pain; he entered pain for us and felt the weight of our pain in a way that we will never know. He lamented, cried, questioned, and even asked God to change the plan.

"Abba Father," he said, "everything is possible for you. Take this cup from me. Yet not what I will, but what you will" (Mark 14:36).

Jesus accepted the pain and endured it. He was crucified for us. But he was also raised to new life for us. There was glory in the pain and glory on the other side of the pain.

There can be the same for you. Today. Right here, right now. It's okay to not be okay.

QUESTIONS FOR FURTHER REFLECTION AND DISCUSSION

1. Why is being honest about our hurt a necessary step toward healing?
2. In what ways have you ever felt rushed in your pain?
3. Take a moment and read John 4:1–8. Jesus was tired and weary from his journey and ministry. In what ways did he demonstrate his need to be cared for by others?
4. Where do you need to practice good self-care right now?
5. Hope reminds us that our current reality is not our final reality. What new beginnings do you sense God leading you toward?

CHAPTER 3

THIS *IS* WHAT GOD IS DOING

Suffering is never convenient, is it? Trials are never timely. Suffering stops your life—it never feels like it fits into your life. We know our battle with cancer was no exception.

As we mentioned, we were heading home from picking up our oldest son, Tyler, when the nurse called. I (Ruth) was driving when Patrick's cell phone rang. It was a quick exchange, but when I glanced over at Patrick writing on a scrap piece of paper, I could see the word "cancer."

It's true that hearing the "C" word is like being punched in the stomach. I wanted to throw up. We both sat in silence. I remember pulling into our driveway and running into the house. Patrick remembers our son getting out and going inside, leaving the two of us talking and crying. Regardless, at some point, I know I hurriedly got out of the car and raced up the stairs to our bedroom.

It felt like a safe place, even if that safe place was just an illusion.

My entire body felt like a balloon someone had just sucked the air out of. I went completely weak. Limp and lifeless. My mind was swirling. I was in complete disbelief. Alone in our room, I googled blood cancer and collapsed to the floor as I read the word "uncurable."

I read it again. Uncurable.

This happens to other people. Not us. How could this be happening to our family?

We never choose suffering. We might say suffering always chooses us. And Patrick and I hoped this was all a mistake. Like someone had accidentally called us with someone else's results.

If that wasn't enough, I felt like we didn't have time for this. This wasn't the plan. It wasn't on the calendar. It wasn't in our life goals. We hadn't scheduled in cancer. I didn't want to learn all about blood cancer. We didn't have time for hours and hours of doctors' visits and tests. We had stuff to do!

Just two years prior, we had moved to Ann Arbor, Michigan, to start a new church. We were in the middle of writing another book. We were raising our four kids.

It was all hard, but fun. Rewarding. Things were good. We had no idea how good they were, until they weren't.

Our suffering felt like an interruption. For us, everything came to a screeching halt. It was an interruption of enormous consequence. It felt like someone severed the life we used to have from the one we were now living. There are some things we walk through in life. And then there are some things we encounter that we just know we will walk with—forever. This was not something that was going to go away, even if we could get through it.

The dictionary puts it rather plainly: an interruption is "a stoppage or hindering of an activity for a time."[1]

But real life is, well, a bit more real. Interruptions, especially from trials, feel more like unwelcome intruders. They stop or hinder our lives. Our normal activity ceases, sometimes for a season and sometimes forever.

The thing with interruptions is we rarely see them coming. Rarely do they announce their arrival. They just hit. Take us by surprise. It's a yearly visit to the doctor. A phone call in the middle of the night. A check-up with a routine ultrasound. One bad business deal. A text message we accidently discover. A spouse's seemingly sudden decision to walk away after decades of marriage. A tragedy, because you, or someone you love, were in the wrong place at the wrong time. A small lump that turns out to be a big deal.

Whatever it is, it always feels like it is getting in the way of our life. The things we want to do. Or think we need to do. And suddenly we find ourselves in a boat in the middle of a lake.

Which is exactly what happened to those first followers of Jesus that we see in Mark 4. The storm hit suddenly. And it must have felt like an interruption to their lives. Something they just needed to get through to reach the other side of the lake.

"The lake," as the Gospels like to call the Sea of Galilee, is located in the Rift Valley—a valley that sits lower in the earth than the mountain ranges to the east and west. As a result, the Sea of Galilee is about 690 feet below sea level. Rain and springs from the mountains in the north flow into the Sea of Galilee, eventually making their way south, toward the Dead Sea.

Because of the surrounding mountains and hills, along with the depth below sea level, weather can be tricky to predict out on the lake. Wind can descend quickly, creating destructive waves and dangerous storms. All rather suddenly. Unexpectedly. The lake the disciples found themselves in the middle of that evening is known for its abrupt weather. It is often the place of storms that brew quietly and then strike quickly. Placid water can turn ominous almost instantly.

Which is exactly what Mark told us happened—a storm interrupted the disciples' trip from one side of the lake to the other. In verse 35, Jesus had promised them safe arrival to the other side. He'd told them, "Let us go over to the other side." So when the storm hit, it certainly must have felt like it was getting in the way of what God wanted them to do. It must have felt like a distraction or disruption to where he was leading them and what they themselves wanted to do.

Isn't that how trials feel? Like they are in the way as we are on the way to something different and better? "Middle" places in our lives are often the hardest. In them it is hard to trust, stay faithful, be patient, have perspective, see the good, and remain close to God.

When Jesus first called some of the disciples, they were casting their fishing nets into the water. They were mending nets on the shore. Dry ground was underneath their feet. When Jesus said, "Come follow me," they followed. "I will make you fishers of men," he told them. We would imagine following Jesus sounded fun. Exciting and full of adventure. It probably seemed like a great work, a work of God, they were signing up for. A lot like when we first believed. We gladly received God's love. We felt his presence. He gave us new identities as sons and daughters. We could see his goodness and faithfulness. Like those first disciples, early in the journey we, too, were excited.

Or maybe Jesus calling the disciples was like when God first called you to a new ministry, a new job, or a new season in life. And yet this journey of following Jesus is full of surprises, isn't it? The path is not always straight. The terrain is not always smooth. Sometimes there is water. And storms. Interruptions, we might say.

But we discover Jesus not only wants to work *through*

us but needs to work *in* us. And this is no secondary work of lesser importance. He doesn't just want to get us from one side of the lake to the other. He uses the "middle."

The storm we are facing is never a threat to God's work; it is often a tool for God's work. Suffering might feel like an interruption to us, but it is instrumental to Jesus.

Undoubtedly, suffering was not God's plan. He hates evil. All of the sickness, pain, disease, loss, and death we experience is the result of Adam and Eve's first sin (Gen. 3). Things are not the way they once were in God's original creation. And they are not what they will one day be when Jesus renews all things and does away with the messiness and brokenness and sin we are all living with. But God can and does use suffering in this life for his redemptive purposes.

Eventually we have to face suffering for what it is. It took me (Ruth) several hours to emerge from our room that first day and about five days of numbness and denial to face our suffering. I hated every second of it. The future felt like walking into the wind. I couldn't wait to go to bed at night. But overmatched and outnumbered, I wrestled every dark emotion that came to visit. And came to win.

Eventually I had to look our interruption in the face. I wanted our old life back. But we all have to step out. Or step up. I had to admit that suffering is not an interruption or parenthesis to our life; this is our life.

This is where God has something else. Something more. Honestly, he has something better for us if we are willing to trust Jesus and turn to him in the storm. Maybe the life behind us is gone. Maybe we fear the one around us is crumbling. The life ahead of us is the life God has given us.

> The loss God allows is always the loss God uses.

Right now, as hard as it may be to believe—or perhaps impossible to perceive—there is encouragement. There is hope. Maybe, instead of us getting our life back, is it possible that God wants to get his life in us? Is it possible that the interruption of whatever trial we are facing is not an interruption at all? What if it *is* the work God wants to do in us? Or needs to do in us?

We know that might be a hard pill to swallow. Because you may think that all God has done is take. Whatever it is you have lost—your health, a job, a loved one, a dream—God is offering you something.

The loss God allows is always the loss God uses.

This is why suffering is not an interruption to what God is doing; it *is* what God is doing. How God meets us and molds us in our suffering is not a lesser work. It is God's greatest work—the work of helping us become who he created us to be.

REMEMBERING THE BIG PICTURE

Years ago, a man in our church went through a significant financial crisis. In danger of losing a lot, maybe losing it all, he felt overwhelmed and paralyzed. He was describing to us recently how everything felt impossible.

He felt abandoned. Alone. Even opening his Bible felt pointless. All he wanted was to get back to his life before the trial. Before the interruption.

We've felt that. You probably have too.

Maybe it's helpful to stop for a moment before we get too far and remember the big picture—step back and ask ourselves who we were created to be and how we were supposed to relate to God. This might help us see what he wants and what he is trying to do in the middle of our suffering. Perspective is always good when pain hits.

The opening pages of the Bible remind us that we belong to God. He is the Creator; we are his creation. Any life we have is from him, and we will one day return to him (Rom. 14:8). We were made to live in relationship with God as a Father, through the Son, and in the power of the Holy Spirit. God is an eternal community of love. A relationship we share in by our faith in Jesus.

In Genesis 1:27, God said something stunning about us. We are made "in his own image." We are made to know God, walk with God, and reflect who he is to the world. We were made to tell the truth with our lives about who God is. This is our fundamental identity. The point of our lives is to point others to Jesus and his kingdom.

We were made to be in a relationship of intimacy, trust, and dependence on God. A relationship where we rule with him and for him. God is our deepest source of being and in him we find real joy and meaning. But it's a relationship we know, from Genesis 3, didn't remain as intended for long.

Sin entered the world from one act of disobedience. One act of distrust. One act of independence. And it changed everything. It brought separation from God. Sin and its consequences invaded every corner of our existence. Everything from cancer to the weeds in your garden is a result of that first falling away.

Life is hard. The struggle with sin and the brokenness in the world is real. We are in a battle. But sin didn't erase the image of God in us—it only distorted it.

And so, when God comes to us in Jesus, he comes to call us home, back to his loving rule, back to himself. Back to life. And back to being fully alive as humans made in the image of our Creator. Our deepest longing and satisfaction is found in knowing and loving God. As Augustine said, "Our hearts are restless until they find their rest in Thee."[2]

Jesus is restoring the image of God in us. He is cleaning us up, if you will, making the image of who Christ is in us more visible. The New Testament tells us that Jesus is the perfect image of God. He shows us, in the flesh, what it looks like to be rightly oriented, rightly postured to God.

> The Son is the image of the invisible God, the firstborn over all creation. (Col. 1:15)

> The Son is the radiance of God's glory and the exact representation of his being, sustaining all things by his powerful word. (Heb. 1:3)

Do you see where this is going? The call to follow Jesus is an invitation to experience abundant life, to be fully alive and fully human. Our goal is to share more and more in the life of Jesus and allow his life to be lived through us.

The apostle Paul said it this way: "My old self has been crucified with Christ. It is no longer I who live, but Christ lives in me. So I live in this earthly body by trusting in the Son of God, who loved me and gave himself for me" (Gal. 2:20 NLT).

This is a process that takes us from "one degree of glory to another" (2 Cor. 3:18 ESV). In other words, God is changing us slowly but surely until one day when we will be fully like Jesus when we see him face-to-face.

We were made to be full of God. Like fish breathe in water, we were made to breathe in God through his Word and Spirit (Eph. 3:16–17, 19) in community with God's people. Growing into this fullness takes time and opening up to more and more of God's love and truth. He wants to dwell in our hearts so that we increasingly experience his life and experience less of our own.

Our lives are often marked by worry and fear and self-centeredness and pride, to name a few. We are prone to wander. We easily drift. Pursue other things. But the life God wants to fill us with is his life—a life that looks like love, joy, peace, patience, kindness, goodness, faithfulness, gentleness, and self-control (Gal. 5:22–23). A life that is marked by trust and steadfastness, even when it feels like all is falling apart.

I (Patrick) don't know if I will live to be an old man, but I want to die a godly man. And that is really what God is after for each of us. No matter what happens *to* us, it's what happens *in* us that is most important because it's the work God is doing in our lives and through our suffering.

While there are many ways we open ourselves up to being filled by more of God, trials uniquely position us to see our need to come to God and be changed by him. We need to keep this in mind as we move on in this book. Otherwise, it's easy to get lost in the weeds and consumed with what is happening *to* us instead of what God is doing *in* us. It's easy to miss who God is inviting us to become.

No matter what happens *to* us, it's what happens *in* us that is most important.

SO WHAT DO I DO RIGHT NOW?

What would we tell you to do right now? With all we've said so far, where would we tell you to begin? We suspect there are a lot of places to start. But the most important place to begin is by looking to Jesus. We know that might seem obvious. But it isn't always that simple.

Right now you are in danger of taking your hurt in a hundred different directions. You are in danger of numbing it. Trying to entertain it away. Minimize it. You are in danger of letting it consume you. Define you. You are in danger of taking your hurt to the wrong person. The wrong relationship. You may very well be in danger of running away from God instead of running to him.

And right now you need to take your hurt to the only one who fully understands it—the one who suffered for you.

In a different story about water in the Gospels, the disciples were once again in a boat. Jesus had left them at sea. He'd gone up a mountain by himself to pray. And Matthew told us in his gospel that the "boat was already a considerable distance from land, buffeted by the waves because the wind was against it" (Matt. 14:24).

"Shortly before dawn," Matthew said, Jesus went out to them (v. 25). In other words, they had been in a boat in the middle of the lake all night. The wind had them pinned at sea. Though they could likely see the shore, they couldn't get there. So Jesus went to them. As he always does, he comes to us when it feels like we can't get to him.

But there is an interesting detail about this water

story, one we probably know all too well from our own experience. When Jesus came walking on the water, the disciples didn't recognize him. In fact, they called Jesus a ghost (v. 26)!

It's hard to see Jesus in the storm, isn't it? It's tempting to run the other way. We want to get out, move on, or go back to life as it was before. We don't always recognize the ways God is present and working in the pain, inviting us to come to him. But ultimately the storms open our eyes to our need for Jesus: to be saved, forgiven, rescued, redeemed, and remade. The swirling winds enable us to see that there is no anchor or hope other than Jesus, who died and rose again for us.

This is what God is doing. The storm is no mere interruption.

Jesus said to the disciples, "Take courage! It is I. Don't be afraid" (v. 27). It's amazing how often in the Bible God tells us not to be afraid. Probably because there is plenty in life to be afraid of! But this is where faith plays its role. In the middle of the storm Jesus invited Peter to come to him, and, for a moment, Peter miraculously took a few steps on the water. He was filled with faith. Then his vision shifted from Jesus to the waves. The water began to swallow him.

Just before Peter sank, Matthew told us that Jesus reached out his hand and caught him (v. 31). Before he rebuked Peter for his lack of faith, Jesus extended his tender touch. It was only then that Peter, along with the other disciples, saw Jesus for who he really was and worshipped him, saying, "Truly you are the Son of God" (v. 33).

As Jesus comes to us, he is inviting us to come to him. To see him for who he really is. This is where growth begins. Not by doing more for Jesus but by treasuring Jesus more because of what he has done for us.

So where would we tell you to start? The first step is always simply coming. Just as we are. With all of the hurt and fears and maybe even the bitterness. Keep coming. Take another step toward Jesus. We're not trying to be like him, just simply desiring to be with him.

Christlikeness is always a byproduct of being with Jesus. The fruit comes as we abide in him, yielding to who he is and what he wants to do in and through us (John 15:1–4). So keep opening your Bible often. Even when you don't feel like it. Especially when you don't feel like it.

Stay on your knees.

Keep taking your tears to Jesus.

Resist feeling like you have to do anything right now.

And simply rest in knowing God is with you. And he loves you.

Remember, suffering is not an interruption to what God is doing; it *is* what God is doing. He is doing it while you feel alone. He is doing it in your waiting and in your grief and in your sickness and in your poverty.

CHANGE *ALL* OF ME

Just over a year before I (Patrick) was diagnosed, I bought a brand-new journal. I was beginning my doctoral studies in discipleship at Biola University. At the time, I had been a pastor for almost fifteen years. So I figured it was time to get more training on how to become like Jesus! Little did I know the kind of education I was about to get.

I flew into Southern California for my first two-week residency. I got in a day early, so before classes began I went to a local bookstore. I wanted to buy a new journal to keep track, in a fresh way, of what it means to follow Jesus. I wanted to memorize his words. Saturate myself with his stories and priorities.

When I bought my new journal, I promptly wrote a short prayer at the top of the first page—a blank page.

It simply reads, "Lord, change all of me."

I underlined the *all*, because it seemed to me there is the stuff we see and the stuff only God sees. And I wanted it all out. Everything on the table. I wanted God to graciously—and gently, of course—transform who I was from the inside out. I wanted to be full of God.

Looking back, it might have been better to start with a different prayer—something safer.

Ruth and I took a walk that week on campus. Directly across from the building where my class was, the construction of a new building was underway. We stopped and watched. And then I added one more prayer.

"Tear me down and build me up again." Like that hole in the ground. Knock the old building down. Dig a hole in the earth. Build a new foundation. And bring a more beautiful structure out of the mess.

Again, in hindsight, perhaps "Lord, bless me" would have been more appropriate!

Not long after this our education would begin. The tearing down would start. The prayer for God to change all of me, and not just some, would be heard. And it would hurt. But it would be good. Something new would begin to emerge.

But we did have to make a choice in our suffering. Here's one of the defining moments. It may not change our circumstances, but it will change how we experience our circumstances. It is the choice to believe God wants good in our suffering.

This act of faith will make or break us. Do you believe God has good for you in your suffering? Or good to bring out of your suffering? We are convinced that if you answer no, your heart will grow cold. But if, by God's grace, you answer yes, your heart will grow warm. Your heart will grow more full of God.

The choice to suffer is never ours. But how we suffer is every bit our choice. And the choice to suffer well is that important.

Pick any verse in the Bible about suffering. We will

find that the bad we are experiencing is tethered to the good God wants to do. One example, a familiar one, is James 1:2–4:

> Consider it pure joy, my brothers and sisters, whenever you face trials of many kinds because you know that the testing of your faith produces perseverance. Let perseverance finish its work so that you may be mature and complete, not lacking anything.

Before we dismiss this passage for being unrealistic or idealistic, keep in mind that the Christians James was writing to were living with the threat of persecution. And poverty. Their lives were increasingly on the line.

God saw fit to remind them that the bad they were about to encounter and were already experiencing was tethered to the good he wanted to do in them.

Those seeds of God's truth and love and grace—the seeds of his promises, the ones we believed so confidently on the shore, the ones we memorized in our quiet time, the ones we journaled about at the coffee shop—they need water to grow. And right now, where it hurts most, where fear is most tangible, where maybe bitterness is taking root, is also the place of a greater work God wants to do. A work in us.

Growth is gradual. And growth is also painful. We always like the promise of growth more than the process of growth. Trials can make us more humble, alive, grateful, compassionate, and open to God.

To be sure, there is much we lose in the storms. We can't imagine what you have lost. Or what you fear you are losing. Everyone's suffering is unique. Not worth comparing. Painful in its own way. But there is also so much we gain, or can gain.

Without making the choice to believe that God wants good and without persevering through the process, we can miss out on what God wants to do. The process of being in the "middle" of the lake is just as important as getting to the "other side of the lake."

We don't mean to suggest God has caused your suffering. He is not punishing you. He's not picking on you like some cosmic bully. What we do mean is that life is hard. Heaven is our future, but sometimes our present hurts like hell. And the Bible makes it clear that God can use what shatters us and make us whole again.

Andrew Murray once wrote that "our heart is the scene of a divine operation more wonderful than Creation."[3] And the apostle Paul said that if "anyone is in Christ, the new creation has come: The old has gone, the new is here!" (2 Cor. 5:17).

God is making us new. He's chipping away at the old. He's molding and refining. Purifying the imperfections. He is testing our faith, proving its genuineness (1 Peter 1:4–7). Will you come to him in the storm? Will you give him just a little bit of room, enough room to begin a new work, one that can be as beautiful as creation itself? It can start right now, when we acknowledge that this suffering is not an interruption. It is what God is doing. And it can be good.

QUESTIONS FOR FURTHER REFLECTION AND DISCUSSION

1. While suffering might feel like an interruption to us, it is instrumental to Jesus. How have you seen the suffering God allowed be the suffering God is using?
2. Take a moment and read Genesis 1:26–27. What does it mean to be made in "God's image"?
3. How is God using your storm to restore his image in you?
4. Often, we take our hurt to the wrong people or places. Instead of turning to God, who or what are you most tempted to turn to in your suffering?
5. What is the difference between trying to be like Jesus and desiring to be with Jesus?

CHAPTER 4

PRY ME OFF DEAD CENTER

We should probably fill in a few gaps about our story. As we mentioned, January 17, 2018, was a turning point in our lives.

The vast majority of people diagnosed with this type of blood cancer are over the age of seventy. I (Patrick) was forty-three. The good news is that the cancer was treatable, even if that treatment wasn't quite like taking a Tylenol for a headache.

First I went through five months of "frontline" treatment, kicking back the cancer considerably. In July I had my first stem-cell transplant—a procedure where they take your good stem cells from you, blast you with a high dose of chemotherapy, then give you back the good stem cells. Almost exactly three months later, I had a second transplant.

In those four months surrounding stem-cell transplants, we spent a total of thirty-five days in the hospital. After each transplant we spent sixty days at home: recovering, avoiding germs, and watching way too much ESPN, HGTV, and Hallmark Christmas movies!

By God's grace and thanks to people praying all over the world, the cancer is in complete remission. According to my specialist, I have had an optimal response, one he generally does not see. Not a trace of cancer remains, but like any cancer, there is always the chance of it coming back.

The crisis is over, but the concern is very much still alive. And so are the ongoing realities of living on maintenance medications designed to keep the cancer at bay. My body will never be the same, and so while "I am fine," I'm not fine. I'm grateful to be alive and grateful for God's goodness. But we live with a new normal, with new limitations and challenges. And, of course, concerns.

At that first doctor's visit, I asked what everyone likely asks when diagnosed with cancer: "How long do I have?" It's one of the memories most vivid in our minds. The specialist, while very encouraging, shrugged his shoulders and said, "I don't know." And then he went on to tell us that this type of cancer behaves differently in different people's bodies.

Even after such a great response to treatment and rapidly growing advances in this area of medicine, we still wonder. We still worry. We still ask the question I asked that first day at the doctor's office.

The truth is the cancer could never come back. Or it could come back in a year, three years, or ten years. It's complicated trying to calculate the effectiveness of treatment and life expectancy when the most common patient is decades older than I am. Because of my age, the statistics out there are not terribly helpful.

And so we live with, "I don't know."

You don't have to have cancer to know what you don't know. Your suffering may be entirely different. Harder. More daunting. But at some level, we are all wrestling with the uncertainty of our lives. The unknown of our circumstance. The "I don't know" how this is going to turn out. Or the "I don't know" why this happened.

We all want certainty. And when we don't have certainty, it scares us. It can harden us. Paralyze us. But the uncertainty has the potential to pry us off dead center too. To realize we are not as strong or as in control as we thought we were. We are forced to stop only looking at ourselves. The "I don't know," whether we like it or not, demands trust.

Trust doesn't come easy for most of us.

If we are to grow and experience abundance out on the water, we have to admit that there are some things none of us know or will know. But what we need most is not certainty or clarity; what we need is trust so we can be transformed.

During those first five months of treatment, we walked almost every day. If you could have recorded our conversations, you would have discovered the content was the same. Every day. I talked about my cancer, and Ruth listened.

I talked to sort it all out. But I talked because I was looking for reassurance. Encouragement. Something new or different for Ruth to say that would make me feel better. Ruth, who is far more like Jesus than I am, finally said one day, "What you are looking for is a statistic. What you need is trust." While I hate to admit it, she was right. What we all need most is not always an answer to why, not a statistic for how long or certainty about the "what if"—we need trust.

> What we all need most is not always an answer to why, not a statistic for how long or certainty about the "what if"—we need trust.

Whether you have cancer, an empty bank account, a child who has walked away from the faith, or a womb that won't conceive, what our hearts need most is trust. And uncertainty can move us from just obeying God to trusting God. There is a difference, as we will see. It's a transition that can be painful but powerful, if we choose.

We think Brennan Manning was right when he said, "Trust is our gift back to God."[1] Sometimes we give that gift of trust slowly, painfully, with tears in our eyes. But when we give it, when we move from just obedience to trust, we move in the direction of transformation.

Trust is not giving up; trust is opening up. Opening our hearts to the possibility that maybe God really does know best. Maybe his wisdom and care and love is what we need most. And so, reluctantly at first, we open our hearts to trust in the middle of what we don't always like or understand. But we open our hearts to a Father who knows best and has our best interests in mind, even if we can't fully comprehend it.

FROM OBEDIENCE TO TRUST

When our oldest son, Tyler, was ten I took him on a father-and-son camping trip. We called it our "Warrior Weekend," based on a short devotional I had written years earlier to help dads raise boys to be godly men. After a night alone in the woods, I wasn't feeling like a warrior. I was feeling like I wanted a warm bed. Hot coffee. Ruth. And air conditioning. But we had memories to be made and lessons to be learned.

On our second night, during one of our planned activities, I wrapped a bandana around Tyler's eyes—hindering his ability to see. He could only listen and pay attention to my voice. Trust my heart. And eventually take some steps.

I began to lead him one small step after another.

Cautiously, he took a step. Then another. In the absence of sight, he'd often put his hands out, grasping for anything to hold on to. Something to steady him. Protect him. And many times he would cry out, asking for more instructions, more help, more "vision." But we made it from one side of our campsite to the other.

Finally, I unwrapped the bandana, exposing his eyes to the path we'd just walked—the one he couldn't see, but had trusted me to lead him down. Then we read the following words of wisdom together:

> Trust in the Lord with all of your heart, lean not on your own understanding; in all of your ways submit to him, and he will make your paths straight. (Prov. 3:5–6)

These words, wise as they are, are not easy to live. And yet, we all will be faced with those moments, those seasons, those storms, where we have to trust what we don't see or understand. We have to "lean not" on our "own understanding."

The struggle to trust and obey is real. But it's also a necessary step toward growth and transformation.

Learning to trust God with what we don't know is essential for being filled with God. If we are to increasingly experience the good life of following Jesus, we have to learn to trust like he did, often with what we can't see or get our minds around.

This is one of the hardest parts of growing and being transformed in trials. Learning to surrender to what Jesus wants—his purposes, and his plans, his wisdom. The Bible talks a lot about obedience. But the obedience God is after is not just an external conformity to what he says. It's an inward alignment of our heart with his, even when we don't understand what he is doing or why he is doing it.

Trust requires humility.

Trust requires saying, "I don't understand, God, but you do."

Trust requires admitting our powerlessness.

Trust requires giving up control. Which maybe is the hardest part. We like control. We like to be at the center of things. We like the comfort it brings us.

We foolishly think we can control God. Even our efforts at obedience are sometimes futile attempts at this. We do good, stay faithful, pray more, give generously, or read our Bibles more frequently in an effort to get God to behave a certain way. Our way. We think if we do xyz, then certainly God will do his part, right?

But our problem is deeper than obedience, isn't it? Our real problem, the problem underneath our obedience, is trust. It's a matter of the heart. Or maybe put more simply, more bluntly—we think we know better than God. This was true of us when we entered the world of cancer. And for our friends who suddenly hit financial turmoil. We know the single mom who called us felt this way shortly after her son was born, lifeless. The wife did, too, when we wept with her in our family room after she discovered her husband was having an affair.

When Jesus took the disciples out on the water and they found themselves surrounded by the storm, they realized they weren't in control. They were helpless. They lacked the resources, the power, the wisdom to fix the situation. They were discovering what we all soon discover, that belief is not just faith in something, belief is faith in Someone. God is at the center. We follow him. He doesn't follow us.

Their first response was fear. They had obeyed him before. But out on the water, in the world of the unknown, they were learning to trust him.

If we don't trust God, inevitably, we will try to be God. And we'll try to control what only he can control. What God is really interested in is our trust.

THE TRUTH ABOUT GOD

So how do we learn to trust God when everything inside us wants to turn from God? We know trust doesn't come easy. And it doesn't come by accident. If we want to trust God, we have to know the truth about him and resist letting our feelings be the facts that define our reality. Most often we have to choose to trust God in spite of how we feel. Our feelings are not always accurate. It's who God is and what he says about himself that is worth trusting. The truth about God, not what we feel about God, is our anchor.

The psalmist said, "Those who know your name trust in you, for you, LORD, have never forsaken those who seek you" (Ps. 9:10).

God's names in the Bible are always connected to his character. His name is who he is. And so the psalmist is telling us something important here. Something that moves us closer to trust. We need a specific kind of knowledge about God to trust him. It doesn't happen just by trying harder. Or having enough faith. Trusting God requires that we know certain truths, which are what make him trustworthy.

The truth about God, not what we feel about God, is our anchor.

When the disciples found themselves in water, they not only encountered a storm, they encountered Jesus. They came to know him in a way they didn't before. Which is why after Jesus stilled the storm, they asked, "Who is this? Even the wind and the waves obey him!" (Mark 4:41). They were discovering the truth about Jesus that enabled them to trust him.

We have to become convinced that he is in control. Right now, when it feels like our world is spinning out of control, Jesus is not scared. Our crisis on earth is not a crisis in heaven. Just as he was in the boat with the disciples, Jesus is unmoved by the waves and water. He is still in charge, ruling and reigning, even in the midst of our chaos.

He really is in control of our finances.

He really can take care of our kids if the worst-case scenario happens.

He really can bring good out of our loss.

He really is involved in what feels like senseless suffering.

One way we've learned to think about all of this is through the lens of bird-watching. This is a hobby we took a liking to several years ago, right around the age of forty. Some of our friends say it is because we are getting old! We prefer *maturing*—the ability to recognize and appreciate beauty. Birds and all.

So, at our house, we currently have six bird feeders, with one more on the way.

One bird bath.

Two bird houses.

And lots of happy birds.

We're not sure how we missed the connection before, but it turns out Jesus likes birds too. In fact, he commanded us to fix our eyes on them so that our hearts might be settled by them. Who knew bird watching was so spiritual?

"Look at the birds," Jesus said, "Your Heavenly Father feeds them. . . . Can any of you by worrying add a single hour to your life?" (Matt. 6:26–27). And then later in

Matthew's gospel, Jesus again said, "Are not two sparrows sold for a penny? Yet not one of them will fall to the ground apart from your Father's will. . . . So don't be afraid; you are worth more than many sparrows" (Matt. 10:29, 31).

There it is again. Jesus telling us to do what feels impossible! He said, "So don't be afraid." Why? Not because there isn't plenty to be afraid of. Not because life always turns out the way we want or wish. Not because all of our prayers are answered. But because of our worth and value to God the Father.

If two sparrows, who are sold for a penny, are loved and well cared for, how much more are we? If that is how our heavenly Father feeds them and sustains them in life, how much more will he do that for us?

But there is more.

Jesus reminded us that God is in control. Even in our chaos. He told us that not one of these birds falls to the ground "outside your Father's care" (v. 29). Not even a bird can fall to the ground or die outside of God's control or care. If he rules over the birds, who are of little value compared to us, how much more is he in control of us? How much more is he truly in control of our circumstances or season of life? How much more is he in control of the chaos swirling around us?

We have a God whose plans and purposes cannot be destroyed. We don't have to be imprisoned by the what-ifs or the I-don't-knows. Worry doesn't have to win. Fear can be silenced. Walking in freedom and joy is possible, not by trying harder but by trusting more. By trusting the truth about God—that he is good and loving and completely in control.

Little did we know that when we took an interest in "birding" it would provide one big lesson every single day: God inviting us to trust him—to have our hearts settled by his sovereign care.

But trusting God requires more than just believing he is in control. It also requires believing he knows best. The psalmist said, "Great is our Lord and mighty in power; his understanding has no limit" (Ps. 147:5).

Did you catch that? If we were sitting across from one another at a coffee shop, we'd encourage you to stop, read it again, and underline that last phrase!

His "understanding has no limit." There is no end to God's wisdom. He sees what we don't see yet. He knows what we are ignorant of. Nothing catches him by surprise. He is not only confidently in control, but he also knows more than we do.

There are many days when our wisdom collides with God's wisdom, crashing into a pile of distrust. We wrestle with our thoughts about what seems best to us versus what God is allowing. And when we eventually surrender to the truth of God's goodness and wisdom, it's another opportunity to let go and open up to him. It's his control and wisdom that nudges us off-center, prying our fingers open one at a time, releasing the control. And letting him be God.

IT'S WHO WE TURN TO IN OUR SUFFERING THAT MATTERS MOST

Every six weeks I (Patrick) go to the hospital for a few hours for an infusion as part of the ongoing maintenance regimen to keep the cancer away. The infusion center is a large room lined with reclining chairs. In each chair is someone fighting a different kind of cancer.

This regular treatment is a constant reminder that we are still in a battle—still in a boat. We have wrestled and resisted the reality that there is much we can't control. There is a lot we don't have certainty on. But what we can control is our choice to trust.

And we trust not what we feel but what God's Word says. Like my treatments, trust is not something we do once and then we are done. It's an ongoing decision we make. It's a choice.

Although our trials have great potential to bring about change in our lives, that isn't always the case. Suffering is no guarantee for growth, because our trials always come with options. We have the option of whether to open up to God and his wisdom, care, and love. It is not suffering in and of itself that changes us; it is who we turn to in the midst of our suffering.

Notice again what the psalmist said in Psalm 9:10: "Those who know your name trust in you, for you, Lord, have never forsaken those who *seek* you" (emphasis added). We don't trust when we feel like it. Often, we trust in spite of how we feel. We trust because we choose to, because we make a decision to seek the Lord. We pursue him in prayer, abide with him through his Word, preach to our hearts the truth of his promises. And the promise is that God will never forsake those who seek him. God gives us his grace, the power of his Spirit, when we seek him.

We can't grow *in* Christ until we give our trust *to* Christ.

CHANGING *HOW* WE SEE *WHAT* WE SEE

Trust from the heart doesn't come easy. We often give our gift of trust back to God slowly and painfully.

We grasp for control. We hold so tightly to everything. Our health. Our family. Our money. You name it, we are all clinging to it. And often for good reasons. And yet God begins to pry us off our need to be in control, to be at the center.

He says to us, *Let me carry this. Let me handle it. I am not just your God; I am the God of generations—the God of Abraham, and Isaac, and Jacob. I am your God and your kids' God and your grandchildren's God. You can trust me.*

We know at first it feels like chaos. But, oddly enough, as we learn to trust God's control and his wisdom and his love, we find freedom in letting go. We find joy in not clenching our fists around what God wants to hold for us. We surrender to God's rule and say as Jesus did in the Garden of Gethsemane, "Not my will, but yours be done" (Luke 22:42).

Trust requires learning *how* to see *what* we see. Things are not always what they seem. We see only in part, don't we? Dimly at times, or maybe not at all.

Learning how to see what we see means we look past what is happening to us or around us. It's learning to see what we cannot quite see yet—that there really is a God who loves us and is for us and is with us. And there really is a God who is waiting for us.

On November 5, 2012, my (Patrick) mom said goodbye to us. We knew her time on earth was drawing to a close, though we had no idea just how quickly that goodbye would come. Just two years prior, almost to the date, we had lost my father in a car accident. With no chance to say goodbye.

Too sick and weak to talk, my mom lay in her hospital bed. Along with my two sisters, I spoke the only words we knew to speak into her ear, hoping and praying they would find their way to her heart.

We were made for life. Death is an enemy—one that will one day be defeated. But we are still forced to face it here on earth. So as my mom's body resisted what is so foreign and unnatural to us and to God's original plan, we wept. And just before she took her last breath, she opened her eyes one last time. And then that was it.

Silence.

A quiet calm.

The feeling that a battle had been fought. And lost.

Or won?

As I thought about my mom opening her eyes one last time, I wondered what she saw. Who she saw.

And then it occurred to me. My mom hadn't just opened her eyes for the last time; she had just opened her eyes for the first time. She was seeing with great clarity what she had longed to see since she first put her trust in Jesus.

She, too, had been seeing dimly since that first time she said yes to Jesus. Now she wasn't taking her last look at earth; she was taking her first look at heaven. She saw what we all are longing to see. Through trials and tears. Through wind and waves. We are looking for what God has promised.

Until then, we see only in part. So we need to remember that it's not just *what* but *how* we see that keeps us moving. Walking. Loving. And trusting.

There is healing in trusting. Healing that leads to God making us whole, more human, more like Jesus. There is joy in letting God be God. There is peace that comes with surrender. There is freedom when, in humility, we trust God's control and wisdom and purposes over our own.

And so, until our last look becomes our first, will you trust God? Will you keep your eyes on Jesus, who even now is perfecting your faith?

QUESTIONS FOR FURTHER REFLECTION AND DISCUSSION

1. What uncertainty are you living with right now?
2. In what ways is trust different than obedience?
3. Take a moment and read Psalm 9:10. What truth about God do you need to remember most right now in order to trust him?
4. How do we often try to "be God" when we choose not to trust him?
5. What area of your life or circumstances do you need to surrender to God?

CHAPTER 5

TRYING TO MAKE SENSE OF OUR SUFFERING

In the early days after the diagnosis, we had plenty of questions. We couldn't help but ask, "Why us?" Or "Why now?" But these were far from the only questions we were asking.

My (Ruth's) biggest questions weren't centered around the why but the how. This diagnosis seemed impossible. My mind couldn't reconcile how this could be happening to us. For years, we'd seen countless people face unimaginable circumstances, never once thinking one day it would be us. *How are we going to get through this? How is this going to affect our kids? How are we going to have the strength?* And the list went on.

I (Patrick) looked at my cancer from every angle. I thought about how I was supposed to be in the prime of life. These years were supposed to be my most influential in ministry and critical working years for earning an income and saving toward retirement. I worried that this disease would not only rob me of my health but rob our family of financial provision and security. And so I struggled with feeling responsible.

I wondered how this sickness would saturate our kids' hearts. Out my front home-office window, I watched as our two sons shoveled our driveway that first winter. My cancer had compromised the strength of my bones, making it too dangerous to lift anything very heavy. So I watched. I wept. Watching my sons pick up wet, heavy snow was a metaphor for the heaviness they now knew and carried thanks to cancer. I felt helpless and fearful.

I thought about Ruth. She was suffering in a unique way—as a wife and as a mom. Her life didn't stop, and I feared the cancer would crush her differently than I feared it would crush me. And, of course, I couldn't help but think of not only losing my battle to cancer but also losing her love for me. Would she love someone else someday if I didn't make it? I was oddly jealous for a love I knew wasn't mine to keep.

We're all trying to make sense of the mess we are in, the water we're in the middle of, aren't we? Your questions may be different from ours, but they are still questions, fueled by hurt and pain and the unwelcome intrusion and interruption of suffering.

One friend of ours is trying to make sense of the death of her daughter. We have family trying to figure out why a promising surgery for their son, who has battled seizures his entire life, failed. A neighbor is wrestling with the loss of his wife from a terminal illness, all the while raising their kids.

There are plenty of questions to go around.

All legitimate questions.

So it's not surprising that as we return to the disciples in a boat in the middle of a lake, we discover that they, too, were asking questions. They were wrestling with what was happening to them. They were trying to make sense of their suffering—like us, their storm had them wondering. Even wavering.

"Is this really what God is like?"

Remember that Mark told us Jesus was asleep while the storm swirled around them. He wrote, "Jesus was in the stern, sleeping on a cushion" (Mark 4:38). I suppose we've all felt that way. Like God was indifferent. Resting. Oblivious to our pain. Our crisis was not really his concern.

Mark went on to tell us that the disciples woke him with a question: "Teacher, don't you care if we drown?" (v. 38).

There it is. Not a question about God's existence, but about his character. The disciples wanted to know if Jesus really loved them in their distress. If he really knew what he was doing. Their chaos seems to be evidence of a lack of care. They were questioning if God was going to come through: a question that had the potential to reshape their faith in Jesus.

That is what storms do. They disorient us. Disrupt us. We've seen friends' faith shipwrecked by storms. But storms also invite us to do something more. It's not enough to stay where we are. It's not enough just to ask questions. As we talked about in the previous chapter, we have to begin to come to terms with the truth: of who God is, of what he is doing, and that maybe he is up to something more in our pain, whether or not we can make sense of it.

This requires that some of our myths or misunderstandings about life and about God get exposed. Part of making sense of suffering is making sense of what is true and what is false. Questions have the potential to lead us down one of two paths: despair or greater devotion. When we see the truth behind both what God is really up to and the myths that we believed, we are in a much better place to move toward greater devotion—to move toward the heart of God.

First, we have to come to grips with the truth that God is up to something far more important than just our comfort.

THE MYTH OF OUR COMFORT

We remember the first car we ever owned that had leather seats with seat warmers and an automatic starter. No longer did we have to dart to the car, chilled to the bone and praying for warmth while waiting for the heat to kick in. It wasn't anything terribly fancy or new, but it transformed our cold winter mornings!

We'll be the first ones to admit we like comfort. Our guess is you do too.

Just listen to almost anyone's conversation and it won't take you long to hear the howling of complaints. You name it, we grumble about it. Traffic. Our child's school schedule. The weather. Our jobs. Family. The church we go to. Not having enough money. All cries of discomfort.

Some of the cries are right and legitimate, tethered to deep sadness, loss, and disappointment. Others are silly and insignificant, clouded by the absence of bigger problems. But on some level we are all comfort junkies. Addicted to easy and convenient. Which is why we hate any intruder that threatens our vision of the good life. But eventually something small, or something big, pokes at our idol of comfort. Discomfort rears its ugly head.

One of the dangers in all of this is that we falsely connect our comfort to God's character. If we are comfortable, then God must be good and loving. If we're uncomfortable, God must be cruel, distant, or, worse, nonexistent.

But as we read the Scriptures, we are increasingly made aware that God is up to something far more important than our comfort. This side of heaven, there is something greater going on than our ease. Each of the disciples would find this to be true. Not only in the boat, but in the rest of their lives.

Our comfort, or lack thereof, is not commentary on God's character.

Maybe you are as tempted as we are to believe the myth that God's goal is our comfort. We can easily buy into the myth that only a comfortable life is the proof of a wise, powerful, faithful, and loving Father.

Our comfort, or lack thereof, is not commentary on God's character.

Again, suffering was not God's idea or plan. He is not trying to make our lives harder than they already are. He takes no delight in what hurts. Instead, he is close to the brokenhearted. He is full of compassion. He hears us. And he is for us. Even in the pain. But God can and does use suffering for his redemptive purposes. For our good and for his glory (Rom. 8:28).

Like any good Father, though, our comfort is not his only goal. Comfort is often an obstacle to the restorative work he wants to do in each of us through the power of his Spirit. God is far more concerned with who we are becoming and drawing us back to the intimate and dependent relationship we were created to live with him. He will often use discomfort, big or small, to bring about real life change, lasting transformation, and Christlikeness.

When the apostle Paul was writing to the church in Rome, he said, "Not only so, but we also glory in our sufferings, because we know that suffering produces perseverance; perseverance, character; and character, hope" (Rom. 5:3–4).

Or, as the psalmist said, "It was good for me to be afflicted" (Ps. 119:71). Why? There was something in the absence of comfort, in the affliction, in the storm, that brought him back to God. And so he said, "It was good for me to be afflicted so that I might learn your decrees."

Cancer is uncomfortable. It is a terrible disease. The suffering is real. It is painful and hard. Horrible in its own right. But, again, cancer is not commentary on God's character. Our discomfort is not evidence of God's lack of love or goodness; he uses it to align our hearts to his. To bring us back to the source of his life, love, joy, freedom, peace, and hope.

We must guard against wrong assumptions about God's goodness and his love. God is producing something in us, even, and especially, when life is hard. Sometimes at first it might feel like he is destroying us. But he's remaking us, casting us into something new and better and more glorious than we were before.

All of this is far easier to accept, easier to believe, when we can see the point in it all. But what about the hurt that seems so pointless?

THE MYTH OF POINTLESS SUFFERING

For many people, these questions of God's love and goodness are not merely philosophical—they are deeply personal. We know they certainly were for the mom of a teen in one of the churches we served at nearly twenty years ago.

Nobody had trained us on how to love someone who was losing her son. We'd never read a book or been coached on how to sit with a dying teenager. We were in over our heads. We'd do anything to go back, knowing what we know now. To sit with her. And to be with her son in hospice care as cancer ran wild in his young body. We won't pretend to know what it was like for her. Or for him. Nor do we pretend to have all the answers now.

What we remember is that it seemed so senseless. Not just painful but pointless. What was God doing? Why was this pain necessary? What good could possibly come out of this story?

And, to be honest, if she had asked us, we wouldn't have had a good answer.

But as honest as these questions and feelings are, they are not entirely built on truth. There is a myth hidden in that mess: because something appears to be pointless, it must be pointless.

Maybe that's your story, your view. You can feel the grief, but you can't see the good. And if this is your story, we know we have to tread lightly. Carefully. We have to ask God to give us the faith to see what he sees. And when we can't see the point in our pain, we have to trust that there really is a purpose.

Do you remember Joseph? The one from the Bible?

His story is a good example of storms that seem pointless but are really purposeful.

Joseph was one of Jacob's sons. He was Abraham's great-grandson. He was also full of pride. Favored by his father, he had a dream. One in which he saw his brothers bowing down to him. Rather than keep it to himself, he shared it with his brothers, who responded as you might expect, with anger and resentment! They would eventually steal his coat of many colors that his father had given him and throw him into a cistern—then sell him to travelers heading to Egypt.

But the Bible says that the Lord was with Joseph (Gen. 39:2). While in Egypt he was taken into Potiphar's house, who was one of Pharaoh's officials, the captain of the guard. Handsome as Joseph was, he was noticed by Potiphar's wife, who pursued him. She not only attempted to seduce him but then falsely accused him of trying to pursue her. Potiphar, outraged, had Joseph thrown in prison. And, once again, the Bible says that the Lord was with Joseph (Gen. 39:21).

Joseph spent years being forgotten and overlooked. Years of wondering what God could possibly be doing. Years of questioning a dream. Years of feeling like God was done with him. Joseph knew all too well the feeling of pointless pain. Questioning whether God was good and loving. And questioning whether there was any real purpose behind all of the heartache and disappointment.

But eventually Joseph would be released. And God would place him in Egypt at just the right time to save many lives during a worldwide famine.

When his brothers came to Egypt for aid, they found more than food. They discovered their brother was still alive. And one of the interesting details the Bible gives us is that just before Joseph revealed himself to the brothers who had caused him so much pain, he "wept so loudly" that the Egyptians heard him (Gen. 45:2).

Have you noticed that small detail before? Why does the Bible record that? What's with Joseph weeping?

Certainly he wept for joy. He wept over the reunion with his brothers. He likely wept, as we do, over how real the pain was. But perhaps he also wept because he finally saw the point in years of what seemed like pointless suffering.

After holding it all in, he couldn't help but let it out. His pain finally had a point. A purpose. One he could see, and was perhaps part of the reason for his tears.

God was with Joseph in the cistern. He was with him in the palace. And we're told he was with him even in prison. At the time, when Joseph felt the pain or disappointment or fear, he couldn't see the purpose in it. He couldn't get his mind around it. We have the advantage, from our perspective, of reading his story and seeing the purpose running like a thread through his story of pain. But Joseph couldn't see it until much later.

Toward the end of Joseph's story we read about

a later encounter with his brothers, when he said to them, "Don't be afraid. Am I in the place of God? You intended to harm me, but God intended it for good to accomplish what is now being done, the saving of many lives" (Gen. 50:19–20).

It's as if Joseph was saying, "I didn't see it then, but I see it now!" Isn't that what we will all say one day? We know we don't always get to see the point right now. For many of us, the purpose of our pain will remain hidden until much later. Maybe Joseph's weeping is a picture of what that day of understanding will look like for all of us. Weeping because the hurt is finally over. Weeping because, finally, its purpose is revealed.

All of the seemingly pointless hurt we experience will be shown for what it truly is. Heaven will reveal the purpose and redeem the pain. Perhaps just before Jesus wipes away every tear, we, too, will weep when he pulls back the curtain on our chaos.

Joseph's story reminds us that even when our suffering seems pointless, it is purposeful to God. But not all of our pain will be resolved here and now.

THE MYTH (AND TRUTH) OF GOOD ENDINGS

So this is how it is going to end? I (Patrick) wondered to myself. When I was diagnosed, I was two years short of finishing my doctorate. In the middle of trying to get a church plant started. We were halfway through writing a book. It all felt like defeat. Failure. I feared that my last chapter would feel like unfinished business.

Isn't this the way suffering can feel? Sometimes the pain and hurt never get resolved. We don't always see the ending—at least the happy ending—the one we all want and are maybe even praying for or expecting.

Instead, the loss or hurt has the last word. And we are left to ask, "How could a good God allow that kind of ending?"

We don't always see the earthly relief from pain and suffering. This is exactly why every story containing a happy ending is a myth, with some truth mixed in. It is both false and true. From an earthly perspective, we don't always see the resolution. The good does not always overcome the bad. Sometimes the suffering feels like defeat. But this is only part of the truth. It's not how our story ends.

This is where the gospel, the good news of God's love, offers us an answer to unresolved pain and loss. It gives us the rest of the truth. The whole truth.

Our story does not end with us; our story ends with God.

The Bible teaches that all human life continues beyond the grave. Life doesn't end with death; the point of our physical death is the beginning of life—forever.

This is why we are regularly told in Scripture to focus

on what is eternal. To "fix our eyes" on the stuff that lasts. The stuff that matters. This life is hard. It's short. But it's not all that there is.

> Therefore we do not lose heart. Though outwardly we are wasting away, yet inwardly we are being renewed day by day. For our light and momentary troubles are achieving for us an eternal glory that far outweighs them all. So we fix our eyes not on what is seen, but on what is unseen, since what is seen is temporary, but what is unseen is eternal. (2 Cor. 4:16–18)

The good news has a good ending. Which is why we shouldn't lose heart.

The good news is that God came among us in the person of Jesus. He suffered, he endured pain, and he even laid down his life for us. But that is only part of the story, part of the truth.

Jesus was raised in power and victory over the grave. Death could not hold him. And his victory will be ours one day. The Bible ends with the great promise of his return to wipe away every tear, do away with death, and finally put all of our lamenting, all of our questioning, and all of our weeping to rest (Rev. 7:17; 21:4).

That is how our story ends—not in defeat but in a glorious victory, in restoration and resurrection.

Making sense of our suffering never entirely solves it. We know you may still have many questions. Legitimate questions. Some that need to be tempered with the truth. And others that may linger, even with the truth, until we see Jesus face-to-face. But more than God giving us answers to all of our questions, he gives us a promise. It's not an *explanation* for our suffering but a promise that he is going to *end* our suffering.

With this promise comes the reminder that while we don't know what the future holds, we know who holds the future. Which is why the end of the Bible pictures Jesus at the center. Right in the middle of it all. Exalted. Lifted up. Worthy. And, above all, worshipped.

It's not an *explanation* for our suffering but a promise that he is going to *end* our suffering.

In that day all of the pain will turn to praise. The weeping will become worship. Once and for all. And so, as hard as it may be, let's start now. Questions and all. Answers or no answers. We don't have to make sense of it all. We need to trust the One who knows everything. Let's look to Jesus and the promise that one day he will make right from all that is wrong.

QUESTIONS FOR FURTHER REFLECTION AND DISCUSSION

1. Take a moment and read Mark 4:38. What question were the disciples really asking?

2. How are you tempted to let comfort, or the lack thereof, be commentary on God's character?
3. How is the story of Joseph an encouragement to you in your storm?
4. According to Genesis 50:19–20, what perspective did Joseph have that can help us in our suffering?
5. In what ways does fixing our eyes "on what is unseen" enable us to deal with loss or hurt?

CHAPTER 6

THE BLESSING OF THE UNBLESSED LIFE

The custom license plate on her minivan read: IMGRMPY. It took a minute to register. But when we read it again, out loud, it clicked.

"I am grumpy."

By the look of things—not her car, but her face—she did look GRMPY. As fellow minivan drivers, we get it. We feel a little grumpy most days getting into our minivan too. Her plate is still one of our all-time favorites.

Looking for personalized license plates is an unofficial hobby of ours when traveling as a family. Most recently, we were behind what we'll just call a really fancy car. Out of habit, our eyes darted to the license plate. But, unlike the minivan, this driver was not grumpy; this driver was blessed. Or at least that's what his license plate said.

It was easy to see why. His car was clean. Fresh-off-the-lot clean. Fast. And expensive. It was likely worth more than our house!

I (Ruth) secretly wondered what would happen if the two drivers had to spend an hour together in the same car, whichever one they chose. One grumpy and one blessed. Maybe they'd hit it off. Or maybe it would be a long, quiet, awkward car ride.

Either way, the point is a lot of people feel "blessed" these days. Especially on social media. And like the fancy car we were behind, the "blessed" life seems to be always connected to success, material prosperity, good health, or some other form of good fortune.

Consider the social media statuses we so often see these days:

- Quiet and sunny day on the beach in Florida. #vacay #blessed
- Another raise? Yes, please! #blessed
- SO excited to begin building the house of our dreams! #blessed

You never read posts like the following:

- Missed our anniversary this year. Too sick from chemo, but discovering what it feels like to trust God with EVERYTHING. #blessed
- Still waiting for Mr. Right. Five years and counting. Learning to rest in God as my greatest Love. #blessed
- Never knew what it was like to long for heaven until now. #blessed

That's just not the norm. And for obvious reasons. It is far better to celebrate what we perceive to be good. Or good for us.

We're not saying God never blesses us with good. We are confident he does, and he certainly desires to do so. Every good gift comes from above (James 1:17). And good gifts from a loving Father can include good health, a pay raise, a college scholarship, or a host of other favorable things.

But the mistake we often make seems to be assuming that *only* those good things constitute the blessed life. The good life. And so the absence of financial security, good health, a loved one, a growing church, a stable family, or a predictable future can easily feel like the unblessed life. A life we want nothing to do with.

We're guessing that whatever you are going through has you feeling unblessed. Your heart aches for a loved one you lost. Or the fear of not knowing if the money is going to be enough to pay the bills is paralyzing. Or you are exhausted, spent in every way, trying to provide care for your son or daughter who has a lifelong disability or disease. You may not feel especially fortunate right now or like you have God's favor, and rightfully so. We can appreciate the desire for the "blessed" life.

But what we've been asking is, What if the unblessed life has a purpose? What if God uses what we think to be the unblessed life to bless us, to give us not a successful life but the abundant life of loving God and others? Even when it's not easy. Or convenient. Or comfortable.

Again, just to be clear, we are not saying suffering or trials are good. They most certainly are not. What we are asking you to consider is that maybe there are certain dangers with the "blessed" life. And Jesus may be using what feels like the unblessed life to show us what the blessed life really is.

THE DANGER OF THE BLESSED LIFE

There are unique temptations in the "blessed" life. Some challenges or obstacles. Some things that might even work against entering into the way of Jesus and sharing in his life.

There's a great example of this in the Old Testament book of Deuteronomy in chapter 8.

For forty years the Israelites had been wandering in the desert. Like water for Jesus' disciples, the wilderness had been a place of trial and testing. The Lord had rescued the nation of Israel out of Egypt and was preparing a new generation of them to enter Canaan—the land of promise.

The desert was hot. Dry. It was the place where things went to die. It was also the place where the Lord humbled and tested his people to see what was in their hearts.

> Remember how the LORD your God led you all the way in the wilderness these forty years, to humble and test you in order to know what was in your heart, whether or not you would keep his commands. (v. 2)

The first five verses in Deuteronomy 8 are about where the Israelites had been. The next fifteen are about where God was leading them. The desert was dangerous. But the promised land would pose an even greater, albeit different, danger.

> For the LORD your God is bringing you into a good land—a land with brooks, streams, and deep springs gushing out into the valleys and hills; a land with wheat and barley, vine and fig trees, pomegranates, olive oil and honey; a land where bread will not be scarce and you will lack nothing; a land where the rocks are iron and you can dig copper out of the hills. (vv. 7–9)

The Israelites were about to experience the "blessed" life. Nothing would be lacking. Abundance was about to be theirs. Prosperity was on the horizon. But so was the potential of forgetting God (v. 11). And the potential for pride or finding satisfaction and security in other, lesser things. This is what's so dangerous about the "blessed" life.

So we read the warning:

> When you have eaten and are satisfied, praise the LORD your God for the good land he has given you. Be careful that you do not forget the LORD your God, failing to observe his commands, his laws and his decrees that I am giving you this day. Otherwise, when you eat and are satisfied, when you build fine houses and settle down, and when your herds and flocks grow large and your silver and gold increase and all you have is multiplied, then your heart will become proud and you will forget the LORD your God, who brought you out of Egypt, out of the land of slavery. He led you through the vast and dreadful wilderness, that thirsty and waterless land, with its venomous snakes and scorpions. He brought you water out of hard rock. He gave you manna to eat in the wilderness, something your ancestors had never known, to humble and test you so that in the end it might go well with you. You may say to yourself, "My power and the strength of my hands have produced this wealth for me." But remember the LORD your God, for it is he who gives

> you the ability to produce wealth, and so confirms his covenant, which he swore to your ancestors, as it is today. (vv. 10–18)

We've all been guilty here, haven't we? We've relied too heavily on our own resources. Gone about our day, our month, maybe even our life with little thought about God. Our security and safety is in what we have built. We've trusted our money too much. And even our joy is elusive—we've tethered it to a hobby, entertainment, the next job, pleasure, a relationship, or even our family.

And so it is no wonder we are warned to be careful of the good life. A friend of ours, Dr. Steven Porter, who teaches at Biola University, helped us see this. We appreciated this truth before cancer, but even more so after. He helped us to see that there are at least three temptations we face when all is good and we are experiencing what we perceive to be the "blessed" life. Yet with these three temptations come three invitations to experience the blessing of the unblessed life.

We wish we could say that we've mastered each of these. But, to be honest, we're still growing and resisting these temptations and fighting for the good life that Jesus offers. Here are three temptations we all need to resist if we want to experience the blessing, the good, of entering into the life Jesus has for us when things feel like they are falling apart.

1. Tempted Toward Self-Sufficiency

The first temptation of the "blessed" life is the temptation toward self-sufficiency—the belief and attitude that we can do life on our own. We might not say it, but the reality is, when things are going as we want, there is often little need for God. We are generally self-sufficient. We have most of what we need.

But then a storm hits. And we realize we are not as strong as we thought. Or as wise as we thought. The resources we possess can't fix what we are facing; it's God or nothing. Which, as it turns out, is where God wants us.

I (Patrick) was scheduled to go see the specialist on a Thursday. We were waiting for test results to come back from Mayo Clinic. When the nurse called on that Monday to see if we were available to come in on Tuesday instead of Thursday, Ruth and I panicked.

"Did the doctor give any indication why he wants to meet earlier?" I asked the nurse.

"No, he didn't," she said.

Of course not! I thought. That would be too easy of a solution for my anxiety. Instead, we would be forced to wait one day to find out why. A day with only twenty-four hours. But a day that felt like an entire year!

In the end, the doctor was doing us a favor by bringing us in early to ease our minds. And while the test results turned out to be serious, it wasn't nearly as serious as we had imagined while waiting.

Waiting, it seems, is one of the ways God teaches us

to depend on him. Waiting forces us to look to God. Seek him. Cry out to him to do what only he can do. This is why waiting on God is never wasted. Whether we are waiting on a doctor to call, a prodigal son or daughter to return, a new job to appear, or a circumstance to change, we are drawn to God in greater dependence.

Waiting brings us face-to-face with reality and reveals our weakness—and also the reality of God's love, wisdom, and power. Waiting helps us to come to the end of ourselves only to find God waiting for us. That's when we experience the opportunity to trade our self-sufficiency for greater dependence.

There is so much in life that is out of our control. There is much we don't know or can't comprehend—it exceeds our wisdom. And there is so much that we have no power to fix or guide or protect. We couldn't change or control what the doctor called to tell us. All we could do was show up and receive whatever it was that God, in his wisdom and love, had for us.

One of the gifts cancer has given us is dependence on God instead of self-reliance. Suffering humbles us and helps us to see we can't do life on our own. In life and death, we are God's.

We are learning more and more just how dependent on God we really are—and really need to be. Suffering either drives us away from God or draws us close to God.

But real life, the good life Jesus promised, a life of increasing love and joy and peace and freedom, is found in dependence. Living in fear and worry is not life—it's death. We were created for dependence on God, not independence from God.

In the New Testament the apostle Paul was not shy about his hardships. He was beaten. Imprisoned. Stoned. He endured poverty. All for the sake of being faithful to Jesus. And yet all of it, he learned, was meant to draw him closer to God. He said it this way:

We were created for dependence on God, not independence from God.

> We do not want you to be uninformed, brothers and sisters, about the troubles we experienced in the province of Asia. We were under great pressure, far beyond our ability to endure, so that we despaired of life itself. Indeed, we felt we had received the sentence of death. But this happened that we might not rely on ourselves but on God, who raises the dead. (2 Cor. 1:8–9)

There it is. That temptation we all face. To "rely on ourselves." Paul told us that his hardships were an invitation not to rely on himself but, instead, to draw near to "God, who raises the dead." The source of real power and wisdom.

While we are often tempted toward self-sufficiency when things are going well, suffering invites us back to

God. We realize we can't do anything on our own. We repent of trying to be God. We admit we need God.

Whatever you are going through, God doesn't want you to go through it alone. The gift of the unblessed life is an invitation to rely not on yourself, but on him. He is still the one who raises the dead. He gives life to the broken and hurting. By his grace, he strengthens. He is close to the humble. And he wants to be close to you if you are willing to draw close to him.

Where in your life are you trying to be God? How are you resting in your own power or wisdom or resources when you should be relying on God?

But this isn't the only temptation we face in the "blessed" life.

2. Tempted Toward Self-Centeredness

We are also tempted toward self-centeredness—the belief and attitude that life is all about us. We are not the center of the universe. What we are learning, though not easily, is that suffering has the potential to teach us to be selfless lovers, opening our eyes and hearts to others.

Self-pity is perhaps one of the sneakiest temptations in our suffering. We can all fall prey to thinking, *Nobody has it as bad as we do.* Suffering is a grind. Emotionally and physically and spiritually. We can feel beat up. Worn out. And overlooked at times. If we're not careful to guard our hearts, we can become consumed with our own trials. This is understandable, and it's probably inevitable for a time. But the blessing in the unblessed life is that, slowly and surely, God is shifting our attention and softening our affections.

Trials can turn us outward. Suffering can help us see that we are not the only ones who exist, nor are we the only ones who are struggling.

I (Patrick) remember calling my sister several months into my treatment. She had faced her own battle with cancer several years before me, but I hadn't realized the extent of her struggle. "I am so sorry," I told her. "I had no idea what you were going through. No idea what you were feeling or thinking."

We were so consumed with our own life. Our own family. Someone else's trial, even someone we loved dearly, was easily overlooked. We didn't share in her suffering until we experienced our own suffering. This, it seems, is part of the purpose of pain. And part of the blessing of the unblessed life. It makes us better lovers. Selfless lovers.

There is a beautiful picture of Jesus in the final hours of his suffering, not thinking about himself but still loving others. Still caring. Admittedly, it is convicting. In a time when everyone should have been ministering to him, he was still ministering to others. Namely, his mother.

The Gospels record for us seven last words of Jesus. And John tells us that one of those cries was out of consideration and care for his mother, who stood at the foot of the cross.

> When Jesus saw his mother there, and the disciple whom he loved standing nearby, he said to her, "Woman, here is your son," and to the disciple, "Here is your mother." From that time on, this disciple took her into his home. (John 19:26–27)

While there is much that could be said about these words from Jesus, one point we can't miss is that even in his hurt, his heart was open to others. Jesus was not just thinking about his own pain. We know this kind of heart, or this kind of capacity for selflessness, doesn't come instantly or easily. But as God grows us and heals us, in time we turn not toward ourselves but toward others.

As we increasingly ground ourselves in God's permanent love for us, we find it easier to give. When the source of love, God himself, becomes our deepest satisfaction, loving others becomes more natural. More pure.

The blessing of the unblessed life is that we are discovering, in new ways, what selfless and sacrificial love really looks like. We are getting closer to the kind of love God has for us in Christ, to loving others without expecting anything in return. It's not that we don't still need others to love us and care for us. But God's love now fuels us to love others more freely.

As we've seen already, we were created for God (Gen. 1:26–27). We were made to reflect him, be his witnesses, and live for his glory. Our purpose for being on this planet is the glorious task of making much of Jesus.

Whether we are blessed or unblessed, the goal is the same: we were created to love God and love others.

The temptation of the "blessed" life is to stay at the center. The invitation, though, is to move off-center and to have our hearts softened for others. To become better lovers. More compassionate. Caring. Gentle. More like Jesus.

But there is still one more temptation we have to resist, and one more invitation of blessing in the unblessed life.

3. Tempted Toward Self-Righteousness

We are tempted toward self-righteousness—the belief and attitude that we deserve the good life.

This is a sneaky one, isn't it? Pride always is. Which is what self-righteousness is. We're usually the last ones to see it in our own hearts and lives.

We were doing an interview not long after we received the news of the cancer diagnosis. And we were asked, "What would you say to the question, 'Why do bad things happen to good people?'" The question is not a new one. And it was asked in general, but also in particular. It was really, "How do you reconcile a good and loving God letting a pastor be diagnosed with cancer? You have given your life to serving Jesus and loving others. Why would God allow good people like yourself to suffer?"

We suppose everyone who is suffering wrestles with thoughts of *Why me?* We certainly did for a time. The answer is simple: we're not that good! Just ask our kids.

They'll tell you the truth. We're all more sinful than we'd like to admit and more unrighteous than we probably even realize.

The temptation we have to resist in the "blessed" life is thinking we are more righteous than we really are. We must resist the attitude of giving to God with the expectation of getting from God. Or thinking, *Because I have done so much for God, shouldn't he return the favor? Doesn't he owe me for all I have done?*

The invitation in the unblessed life is to see Jesus as righteous. Where we have been unfaithful, he has been faithful. Where we have been disobedient, he has been obedient. Where we have been impure, he has been pure. Where we have failed, he has succeeded.

> God made him who had no sin to be sin for us, so that in him we might become the righteousness of God. (2 Cor. 5:21)

We don't deserve God's love. But while we were still sinners, Christ died for us (Rom. 5:8). That's the good news. And if Christ never gives us anything more, he has already given us more than we deserve. He has met our greatest need—the need to be forgiven. The need to be reconciled with him. The need to know and experience that intimate relationship we were made for—the one our hearts really long for.

All is a gift. And whether we feel blessed or unblessed,

we know that Christ is in us and we are in Christ. A gift we didn't earn and don't deserve. And a gift that nothing can take away.

Good health. A well-paying job. A stable family. Career success. They are all good gifts. We should be grateful, give thanks, and praise God for them. But they can't replace God. They can't be the source of our deepest joy, satisfaction, or security.

If we have Jesus, we have everything. Which means we can lose everything and still have it all.

If we have Jesus, we have everything. Which means we can lose everything and still have it all.

Part of God changing and growing us involves us realizing that prosperity can be far more dangerous to our soul than pain. These temptations of the "blessed" life can lead us away from God, the source of lasting joy and hope. Trials enable us to see how the unblessed life is really the "blessed" life. While we lose much in suffering, we can gain far more.

EMPTIED TO BE FILLED

If we search the New Testament, we quickly discover that the words *blessed*, *bless*, and *blessings* occur frequently—over one hundred times. And we also discover that being blessed is never the same as having plenty of money in the bank, health, or an absence of tears.

In Scripture being blessed is most often associated with persevering in trials, promises of God, or the benefits of belonging to Jesus in faith. Take a look at the following examples:

> Looking at his disciples, he said:
> "Blessed are you who are poor,
> for yours is the kingdom of God.
> Blessed are you who hunger now,
> for you will be satisfied.
> Blessed are you who weep now,
> for you will laugh.
> Blessed are you when people hate you,
> when they exclude you and insult you
> and reject your name as evil,
> because of the Son of Man." (Luke 6:20–22)

> Blessed is the one whose sin the Lord will never count against them. (Rom. 4:8)

> Praise be to the God and Father of our Lord Jesus Christ, who has blessed us in the heavenly realms with every spiritual blessing in Christ. (Eph. 1:3)

> Blessed are the dead who die in the Lord from now on. (Rev. 14:13)

> Why? Because "whether we live or die, we belong to the Lord." (Rom. 14:8)

Blessings, then, are not all of the things that make our lives easier or happier. To be blessed is to have God's favor through our faith in Christ. To be blessed, or happy, is to know the deep joy of being fully satisfied in God. A delight that no circumstance can take away.

And so the good life, the blessed life, is sometimes the unblessed life. The life and circumstances and seasons that cause us to draw near to Jesus in new ways, deeper ways. That cause us to delight in him alone. The pain allows us to cry out to him, seek him, find hope in him, and rest in him in ways we never did before.

This is the abundant life, the good life Jesus promised. It's not a successful life, but it's a life that's full because it's full of God.

> The thief comes only to steal and kill and destroy; I have come that they may have life, and have it to the full. (John 10:10)

God wants to fill us. He wants to chip away at the tough soil of our hearts. Then when our hearts are soft and open, he is able to fill us with more and more of who he is. This is God's heart for our heart: that we "may be filled to the measure of all the fullness of God" (Eph. 3:19).

But to be filled, we have to be emptied—something

Jesus does in the unblessed life. And when we are emptied, in increasing ways we come to realize what the blessed life really is.

The blessed life is not what we *get* from God; it is the life we live *with* God.

QUESTIONS FOR FURTHER REFLECTION AND DISCUSSION

1. According to Deuteronomy 8, what dangers exist when we are experiencing the blessed life?
2. What were God's people instructed to do to guard their own hearts?
3. In what area of your life are you most tempted toward self-sufficiency?
4. Explain how your suffering has either turned you inward or outward.
5. In what ways do you think the blessed life is not so much what we *get* from God but the life we live *with* God?

CHAPTER 7

WE ARE NOT ALONE

"I'm so sorry. There's no heartbeat," the doctor said.

I (Ruth) felt like I heard my own heart stop from the news that the baby inside of me was no longer alive. And this happened not once, but five times over a ten-year time period. I can't begin to explain the deep anguish that was stirred up over and over again, with no explanation as to why I kept losing my babies. Every time I was pregnant, a wet and heavy blanket of fear surrounded me. With no comfort, this blanket covered me. And nothing seemed to lighten the load.

I felt so alone. And at times, God felt so distant. I couldn't help but wonder, *God, do you love me? Because this doesn't feel like your love. It's not supposed to be this way.*

Suffering can be lonely. And God can feel far away.

We can feel alone in our suffering, because each of

our trials are unique. How I suffered is different from how Patrick suffered and how you are suffering, which can make us feel desolate in our chaos.

But the worst pain of all, the darkest suffering, is when even God feels far away. Distant. Uninterested. Uninvolved. The most profound hurt is when God himself seems to have left us. We think we have to get through this storm and suffering alone.

Let us stop here and encourage you with a simple truth: you are not alone in feeling alone. You are not the first person to walk through suffering or hardship and wonder whether God is for you or against you. If you are struggling with feeling like God is absent, nothing is wrong with you. The feeling is not a weakness or a sign of your lack of faith.

The Bible tells us that God is always present:

> Never will I leave you; never will I forsake you. (Heb. 13:5)
>
> > If I go up to the heavens, you are there; if I make my bed in the depths, you are there. (Ps. 139:8–9)

But that doesn't mean we are always aware of his presence. We don't always sense it. This is where we have to be careful of beating ourselves up. Treating ourselves too harshly as if something is wrong. This is seemingly another way God meets us and changes us in our storm.

First, though, remember we are not alone in feeling alone. Let us explain with a few examples.

One of the most brilliant and influential minds in Christianity felt alone. C. S. Lewis wrote a short book, more of a journal turned into a book, called *A Grief Observed*. In it he talks through his pain and suffering and doubt after his wife's death.

> Go to Him when your need is desperate, when all other help is vain, and what do you find? A door slammed in your face, and a sound of bolting and double bolting on the inside. After that, silence. You may as well turn away. The longer you wait, the more emphatic the silence will become.[1]

Lewis describes what we have probably all felt: this strange sense that God is not there when we need him most. The silence, as Lewis described, was like God slamming a door in his face. He, too, felt alone.

Consider another example.

Come Be My Light is a collection of the private writings of Mother Teresa, best known for her lifelong work among the poorest of the poor in Calcutta.

One of the things you notice as you read her writings is the different seasons and circumstances in which she felt alone and struggled to feel God's presence. She was often deeply troubled by what she thought to be a lack of God's closeness. She struggled to feel him or discern his voice.

Notice some of the language she used to wrap around her loneliness: "This untold darkness—this loneliness—this continual longing for God. . . . The place of God in my soul is blank."[2]

So here is where we have to fight. Here is where we have to trust that what God says is true, whether we feel it or not. And the greatest truth we need to hold on to is that we are not alone. God does not leave those he loves. And he loves us more than we know.

But if we are to let that truth encourage us—and even change us—we have to understand that God's love is more than just what he feels; it's what he does. It's how he acts toward us, whether we can perceive it or not.

One of our favorite examples of this truth is Psalm 107: a story about water, storms, and feeling alone. But most importantly, it's about God's loving action toward those in distress. And just how far he will go to be near, with, and for those he loves.

GOD'S LOVE IN OUR LONELINESS

The book of Psalms is full of praise. But also, as we talked about in chapter 2, it contains laments, or honest cries of the heart. Questions, much like ours. Prayers and songs and questions that bubble up and overflow from feeling alone, confused, or disoriented.

Similar to Mark 4, Psalm 107 describes a boat trip

gone bad. Like the disciples, the subjects of this psalm were some who found themselves surrounded by water in a situation so severe that they thought for sure they were going to die (vv. 23–27)!

"Then"—also just like those disciples in Mark 4—"they cried out to the LORD in their trouble" (v. 28). They, too, felt all alone. Fearful. Wondering if God cared. But then we are told that God did not leave them. The psalmist said, "He brought them out of their distress. He stilled the storm to a whisper; the waves of the sea were hushed. They were glad when it grew calm, and he guided them to their desired haven" (vv. 28–30).

The Lord was with them. Fighting for them. Going after them. Pursuing them and protecting them. Right there, in the middle of a storm, they were not alone.

Which is why, four times in this psalm, we read the phrase, "Let them give thanks to the LORD for his unfailing love" (vv. 8, 15, 21, 31).

Did you catch that? We are to give thanks, because God's love is "unfailing." His love "endures forever" (v. 1). The psalmist wanted us to know that who God has been, he will continue to be—namely, full of love. And not even the fiercest of storms, the darkest suffering, or the most painful trial can stop God's love for us.

Both Ruth and I (Patrick) love HGTV, good coffee, Michigan football, and a host of other things. But the kind of love the Bible speaks of is different. Deeper. While it's true to say God "feels" for us, his love is so much greater. More robust. All encompassing. More than affection, it is action. It's not just a sentimental love; it is a sacrificial love.

He has *hesed* for us.

Hesed is a word used hundreds of times in the Bible. It refers to God's devotion, loyalty, faithfulness, truthfulness, and dependability. Again, it's not just how he feels about us; it's his character. His actions. It describes the lengths he has gone and will go to keep his promise to us. His *hesed*, his love, is loyal.

And because God's love for us is loyal, we can have assurance that what God has been, he will continue to be. We can count on his love. Jesus will be in the future what he has been in the past.

"The LORD's unfailing love surrounds the one who trusts in him" (Ps. 32:10). So if you are feeling alone and disoriented by where you are, remember that it is God's love that holds you there. It sustains you, working for your good and accomplishing his purposes. Charles Spurgeon once said it this way: "Had any other condition been better for you than the one in which you are, divine love would have put you there."[3]

And so we have to trust that there is nothing that comes into our lives that does not first pass through the love of God. His loyal and faithful love will not leave us.

One of our favorite promises from God is found in Isaiah 43:

> When you pass through the waters, I will be with you; and when you pass through the rivers, they will not sweep over you. When you walk through the fire, you will not be burned; the flames will not set you ablaze. For I am the LORD your God, the Holy One of Israel, your Savior. . . . Do not be afraid, for I am with you. (vv. 2–3, 5)

We have to continually remind ourselves of not just *what* we are up against but, more importantly, *who* is with us. Through Jesus, God has given us the hope and assurance that he will never leave us or forsake us. The future is his. And while God does not promise us a future without pain, he does promise us a future with his presence.

On shore or in the water, God's love never leaves us. What God has been before the storm, he will be in the middle of it. What he was when we were on the shore, he will be out in the water. His love has not left us. And whatever is before us—down the road, farther in the waves—God's love has not and will not leave us.

What God has been before the storm, he will be in the middle of it.

Just because we *feel* alone doesn't mean we *are* alone. When chaos is our classroom and the darkness lingers, one of the greatest lessons we need to learn is that we are not alone, and we are loved.

LONELINESS LEADS US TO THE LOVER

When we are hurting, we often struggle with the perceived absence of God. But the truth is different than our perceptions. God often takes us into the dark to help us discover our false loves—the things we look to for our happiness, security, or hope. These false loves get dislodged so that we might attach ourselves to Love itself. Real Love. Everlasting Love.

St. John of the Cross first wrote about this experience called the "dark night of the soul" in his poem by the same name. We'll come back to this in just a moment. But first, it is worth pointing out that later writers would observe that there are stages of the Christian life, different "seasons" we move through, although not always just once or even in order.[4] In each part of the journey, Jesus is doing something new, different, and necessary.

We all begin by experiencing the first stage, the *Converted Life*. Here the lifelong journey of trust in Jesus starts. We have experienced God's love and forgiveness. There is a new birth. The Holy Spirit gives us a new nature, with new longings and desires. We begin to wrap our lives and priorities and pursuits around Jesus and his kingdom.

Growing gradually, we enter into the *Learning Life*, or what we might call the grounded life because it is when our new faith begins to grow deeper roots. We have a strong desire to know and learn and obey.

Stage three is the *Active Life*, the stage or season in

our walk with Jesus when we put our faith into action. We discover our unique gifts and how to serve others. Taking action is a priority. We attend church regularly and give and serve often. Pouring ourselves out for others is the mark of maturity in this stage. But the danger is that serving God is not always the same as knowing God.

And here is where things get messy. Things get wet. The descent begins. Somewhere around stage three a crisis strikes. A storm surrounds us. We experience loss. Pain. Confusion. Disappointment. And we find ourselves in new territory. This next stage, if we choose to enter it and learn from it, has been called the *Inward Life.*

Whether you agree with these stages of life or not, we all eventually experience the "dark night of the soul." This is a season or circumstances when we feel alone, abandoned, and scared. God isn't making sense. Our Bible answers don't work—or at least not as easily. And we might even think God is absent. But God never leaves us. He does not forsake us.

So what is he doing?

Thomas Merton once wrote that "God who is everywhere, never leaves us. Yet He seems sometimes to be present, sometimes absent. If we do not know Him well, we do not realize that He may be more present to us when He is absent than when He is present."[5]

Merton is saying that when God feels absent, he is more present than we realize. There is a purpose when he is distant.

Loneliness is meant to bring us back to the Lover.

The "dark night," or whatever language you prefer, is meant to purify our love for God. It's part of the journey. The hurt but also the healing. The trial but also the transformation. Maybe in the past we've loved God and served him for what he's done for us. We've loved the Giver but really we love the gifts. And so the feeling of God's absence purges us. Refines us. Our hearts get exposed along with the things we hold to that are lesser loves. And we discover parts of us that maybe don't love God. Or trust him. Or delight in him.

As our hearts are laid bare we can choose to lean into this realigning season and learn what it is to love God for who he is and not just what he does. We discover that walking with God does not mean always understanding him, but still ultimately being drawn to worship him.

And then, as we begin to see and know God more deeply as the source of an everlasting and unending love that we cannot be separated from—even if life strips us of everything—we are drawn back to him and the beauty of his heart. We're able to say what the psalmist said, "Whom have I in heaven but you? And earth has nothing I desire besides you" (Ps. 73:25).

Remember that the loneliness is meant to lead us to the Lover. Because, after all, God's love that endures forever is what our souls need most, and it's the only thing that lasts forever.

WE ARE NOT ALONE, NOR WILL WE EVER BE

We suppose there are a million and one things that run through someone's mind when storms hit—when you find yourself in water. And yet you also find yourself in a fog. Or blur.

We were sitting in our family room when we received a phone call. I (Patrick) had just returned from seeing my mom in the hospital. Just days earlier, she had been admitted to a local hospital about twenty-five minutes away. Her lungs were tight. Exhausted. Searching hard for air because of pneumonia. She was not doing well. But at least she was stable, or so we thought. And then the phone rang.

"You better come back here," one of my sisters said—I'm not sure which. Her voice sounded familiar but felt foreign. This is how pain always feels: out of the norm, alien.

I acted before really thinking. Before I knew it, I was with my mom. Beside her. Holding her hand. In hindsight, there is much I'd do differently. But none of that matters now. And I remember doing what anybody would do in that situation, when you know the end is near.

I told her I loved her. I'd tell her more now if I could. But what I regret the most is that I let go of her hand. My sisters had been with her much longer. Laughing, talking, and sharing stories. But they had slipped out into the hallway for just a moment.

I let go of her hand for just a moment. Long enough

to go out and find my sisters. And by the time I found her hand again, she had let go. No longer strong enough to hold on or conscious enough to know she was being held.

For months the guilt and regret of letting go of my mother's hand too soon haunted me.

When Ruth and I were in college, we had memorized Psalm 139, a passage of scripture we'd come back to often over the years. It's a reminder of God's goodness and faithfulness and love. Like I had done so many times before, I began to recite those words in the months after my mom passed away.

> You hem me in behind and before,
>   and you lay your hand upon me.
> Such knowledge is too wonderful for me,
>   too lofty for me to attain.
> Where can I go from your Spirit?
>   Where can I flee from your presence?
> If I go up to the heavens, you are there;
>   if I make my bed in the depths, you are there.
> If I rise on the wings of the dawn,
>   if I settle on the far side of the sea,
> even there your hand will guide me,
>   your right hand will hold me fast. (Ps. 139:5–10)

If you read those verses again, slowly, you'll notice the psalmist mentioned God's hand three times.

God's hand was upon him.
God's hand guided him.
God's hand held him fast.

One night, as we were driving home from where my mom had lived in the last few months of her life, the Holy Spirit brought this passage to mind. Quietly I began to say God's Word out loud. And it was like God was whispering his Word to me: *When you let go, I didn't.*

Almost instantly the regret was gone. And in its place, the reminder. The promise. Not just for me, but for all of us who have let go—or struggled to hold on. The hand of God, God's love and faithfulness, never lets us go.

God holds us even when we struggle to hold on to him.

The greatest example of God's unending and loyal love is the cross. The place where Jesus felt like he had been abandoned. The place where God the Father felt distant. Hard to perceive. Impossible to feel. The place where Jesus cried out, "My God, my God, why have you forsaken me?" (Matt. 27:46).

God holds us even when we struggle to hold on to him.

Jesus endured the feeling of being forsaken and abandoned so that we would never be forsaken or abandoned. We are not alone.

> For I am convinced that neither death nor life, neither angels nor demons, neither the present nor the

> future, nor any powers, neither height nor depth, nor anything else in all creation, will be able to separate us from the love of God that is in Christ Jesus our Lord. (Rom. 8:38–39)

DO YOU LOVE ME?

God answers our question, "Do you love us?" with a resounding, "Yes!" But God also asks us a question. He is inviting us to open up to him by asking us, "Do you love me?" (John 21:15).

Here's where more growth comes. More transformation happens. By God's grace, we need to begin to say, "If you loved me in your suffering, Jesus, I will love you in mine." One "yes" at a time. As we follow Jesus there are countless opportunities to say yes or no. Out on the water, in the water. More choices. More chances.

Maybe this is a good time to temporarily put this book down. Not because the chapter is over. But because you need to stop reading and simply tell Jesus yes.

"I might not understand what is going on, but I say yes."

"I may not be able to feel your presence, but I say yes."

"I can't feel your love right now, but I say yes."

Yes to surrendering to you, God. Yes to staying faithful to you. Yes to obeying you. Yes to letting you meet me and change me and grow me into who you want me to be. Yes to loving you, because you first loved me.

QUESTIONS FOR FURTHER REFLECTION AND DISCUSSION

1. Take a moment and read Hebrews 13:5 and Psalm 139:8–9. Why is this promise so important to remember in our storms?
2. Why is it important for us to guard how we respond when God seems distant?
3. What "lesser loves" are you discovering in your suffering?
4. How is God using your storm to lead you to delight more in his love?
5. In what ways is Jesus asking you to say yes to him in your suffering?

CHAPTER 8

DISCOVERING WHAT WE REALLY BELIEVE

It was June 2018 when we flew to California so I (Patrick) could finish up my last residency for my doctorate. Ironically I was finishing my graduate studies in discipleship, what it means to follow Jesus. I'm supposed to have this stuff figured out, right? But I didn't. And I still don't, completely.

There were about twenty-five students in my cohort. We sat in rows that first day. Most of us hadn't seen one another since the previous summer. And so we took turns, one by one, sharing what was new. Victories and defeats. The good, the bad, and the ugly. Then we shared what Jesus had been teaching us.

I'm an introvert; social gatherings always make me a

little sweaty (Ruth, as an extrovert, lives for them). So I groaned inwardly at having to share publicly, in front of the whole class, what I had been learning privately.

Most of my classmates knew about my diagnosis. So when it came time for me to share, I felt a bit of pressure. Maybe it was pressure I was putting on myself. Maybe not. But sometimes when someone goes through something deep and hard, we assume they've gleaned some new and profound insight. I hadn't. At least not the kind typically expected.

I could feel the letdown coming as my time to share came closer!

Avoiding as many Christian clichés as I could, I shared what felt more like a confession than an announcement. In a nutshell, this is what I said:

"What I am learning is not terribly profound. It's not terribly deep. But it is deeply concerning at times. If there is anything I have learned in this storm, it is that I am not as strong as I thought I was. I don't have as much faith as I thought I did."

Well, there it was. Out in the open.

That was it. Nothing worth putting on a coffee mug, bumper sticker, or Christian T-shirt. Just the simple truth that suffering often locates us: puts us on a map and shows us exactly where we are. It exposes us, as we mentioned in the last chapter. It shows us the hard truth about our hearts, revealing what we really believe and even sometimes what we don't yet believe.

NOT AS STRONG AS WE THINK WE ARE

We are guessing you have had a similar experience. We know it can be hard to admit, maybe a little embarrassing to confess, that what you believed so confidently on the shore collapsed and fell apart out on the water. It's the kind of stuff that perhaps you feel comfortable telling Jesus, but not your friend or mentor. Or small group. Or Sunday school class. And for me, not a class full of fellow ministry leaders. But it was, and still can be, the truth.

When we return to the boat, the one the disciples were in, we'll notice this is exactly what happened to Jesus' first followers. Which should be some comfort to us, but also a challenge.

As you know by now, when the storm hit suddenly and unexpectedly, the disciples panicked. They felt paralyzed. They questioned Jesus. Then they cried out to him. Mark told us that the storm was real, not a figment of their imagination. They weren't just being dramatic!

"The waves broke over the boat, so that it was nearly swamped" (Mark 4:37). This was no small storm. They had plenty to be afraid of.

But if we look closely, the waves weren't their real problem. There was something far more dangerous than the storm and the waves and the water. The real threat was not what was happening *to* them but what was going on *inside* of them. A threat that only a storm could bring to the surface.

Their lack of faith, or insufficient faith, was more dangerous than the furious storm. They were not nearly as strong as they thought they were. There were pieces or places of unbelief that only a storm could reveal.

Jesus wanted to replace their fear with faith. Let's take a closer look at what he said to them after he miraculously calmed the wind and the waves: "Why are you so afraid? Do you still have no faith?" (Mark 4:40).

Jesus' question certainly resonates with us. It also stings a bit, doesn't it? It's a little too close to home. A little too close to our hearts.

"Do you *still* have no faith?"

Before Jesus gets to their faith, he used the word *still*. Why? Mainly because the disciples had already seen Jesus in action. He'd proven himself before. They'd been with him when he drove out demons and healed the sick. With their own eyes, they'd seen Jesus

- deliver a man from demonic possession in Capernaum (Mark 1:21–28);
- heal Simon Peter's mother-in-law from her fever (Mark 1:29–31);
- touch a leper, showing that he is not only able to heal but willing to (Mark 1:40–42);
- tell a paralyzed man his sins were forgiven and then command him to get up and walk (Mark 2:1–12); and

- tell a man with a shriveled hand to stand up so everyone could see as he healed him, on the Sabbath of all days (Mark 3:1–6).

So it's easy to see why Jesus used the word *still*! They had certainly seen and heard enough. They knew enough to know better. At least with their heads. That's the toughest journey. But if we are going to be transformed in our trials, our faith has to move from our heads to our hearts.

The disciples still had no faith. But no faith in what? What was different this time? For sure, they still weren't seeing Jesus for who he was. But that's not all.

In every experience and every example, Jesus was coming through for someone else. He was delivering and restoring and sustaining others. The difference this time is that the disciples had faith that Jesus could come through for others but lacked faith that he would come through for them.

> If we are going to be transformed in our trials, our faith has to move from our heads to our hearts.

There is a running joke in our house that Patrick is the king of singing lyrics wrong. It doesn't matter the song. Ones he has known for years, even decades, he still has a unique ability of twisting and distorting. Sometimes in heretical fashion. To the point that our kids don't know if he is joking at times. Unfortunately, he's not!

Recently, I (Ruth) caught him again. He was singing a favorite worship song of ours about God's love and goodness. The problem was that when Patrick mixed up several of the lyrics, he was singing about God's saving power and goodness toward others, and not himself!

He had replaced every "me" with "you." Not only does the song not make sense that way, it has God's goodness chasing after someone else instead of Patrick!

It's a very different song when you think the love of God and power of God is for others instead of yourself. And it's a very different storm when you believe God's goodness is chasing after others instead of you. Or that the kindness of God is only available to someone else. This is one of the mistakes Jesus' followers made out on the water.

They had faith for others but lacked it for themselves.

They believed Jesus could deliver a man possessed with an impure spirit. His goodness could restore a leper. His power could make a lame man walk. A blind man to see again. A mute to speak. But when it came to Jesus' goodness and power saving and sustaining them in the storm, they had no faith. It was their lives on the line, not someone else's. It was their skin in the game. And they doubted.

It turned out they were not as strong as they thought they were.

Maybe right now you are in that place. Disoriented by your chaos. Confused by what God is doing. Or not doing. Devastated by what he is allowing. Perhaps skeptical because he hasn't come through when and how you thought. You've seen his goodness in someone else's life, but you doubt he can show his goodness to you.

Here's where we raise our hands and say, "Me too." That's us. We've seen God be faithful. We've tasted his goodness. We have sought the Lord, and he was not silent. He was not far off. And yet we can still have such little faith.

For us.

But maybe this is one of the purposes of suffering. Part of the process. More transformation in the trials. A chance to see what is really inside. Not what we say we believe. Not what our head thinks. But what our hearts trust.

We've mentioned *A Grief Observed* by C. S. Lewis already, but one of the other things he points out is that we never truly know the strength of a belief until it is tested—until its truth or falsehood is a matter of life and death to us. It is one thing to claim a belief, but quite another to cling to it.

Using the illustration of a rope, Lewis wrote, "It is easy to say you believe a rope to be strong and sound as long as you are merely using it to cord a box. But suppose you had to hang from that rope over a precipice? . . . Only a real risk tests the reality of a belief."[1]

That's one of the things chaos and not a classroom does: it allows us to get under our fear and our worry and control and comfort to discover what we really believe. Or don't believe.

A "real risk," though, reveals real faith.

The Bible refers to this process as refining and often uses the imagery of gold being purified. When gold is dug up and taken from the earth, it is far from perfect or precious. Soil and minerals and other metals are typically attached.

Gold has to be sifted. Heated. For what purpose? So that the impurities can be separated out, leaving what is good and what is pure. This is the imagery Peter used in the New Testament. A picture that was all too real for him, as he himself had been through plenty of refining moments with Jesus.

Much of what is really in our hearts is hidden without heat. Pain and loss and suffering "bring to the surface" impurities of our faith. "Pieces" of sin and unbelief can linger for years without storms. And so this is the gift of going through something hard.

Trials prove how genuine our faith is. They help test the quality of our belief, refining it in the process. Peter wrote, "These [various trials] have come so that the proven genuineness of your faith—of greater worth than gold, which perishes even though refined by fire—may result in praise, glory and honor when Jesus Christ is revealed" (1 Peter 1:7).

Our faith, when refined and deepened, is of greater worth than gold. It sustains us. Gives us hope. Allows us to be still. Remain joyful. Keep pressing on. But it will one day perish. There will be no more need for it. And the promise is, when we persevere in faith, keep going and believing and trusting, there will be praise from Jesus.

What we need right now, though, is to see clearly. To get a better glimpse of our hearts. To see belief and cling to it but also spot unbelief, so we can turn from it.

A GOOD PLACE TO ASK QUESTIONS

I (Ruth) didn't realize what it felt like to lose financial security and totally depend on God. That is, until we were caught between insurance companies. Or, I should say, caught without insurance. The timing could not have been worse.

It was shortly after we moved to Ann Arbor when Patrick began experiencing heart trouble: his heart rate would become not only irregular but dangerously high. Looking back, it may very well have been connected to his cancer. But the point is, because of our lack of insurance we were suddenly at risk of losing a lot. Almost overnight, we became responsible for medical bills totaling tens of thousands of dollars.

My eyes were opened to others who found themselves in financial desolation. I had an all-new appreciation for the struggle that keeps you up, wide-eyed, in the middle of the night, wondering how on earth you are going to make ends meet.

For me, this storm revealed what I really believed. And didn't believe. In that achingly long season, God showed me that I could trust him. Although it was scary, I was able to witness the miracle of friends who sent money and ways that God provided, even when it seemed impossible. For the first time that I can remember, we were completely vulnerable with no other option but to anchor our security in the God who meets us in our chaos.

This is a good place to start asking questions. Questions of our own hearts. Questions like:

- Who or what am I looking to for my security?
- Where am I taking my pain?
- What is my hope anchored in?
- How much do I believe that Jesus conquered death?
- Do I trust God's promises?
- What sin was hidden, but is now revealed in the heat?
- Do I believe that God is good?
- Do I trust that God is in control of all things?

The disciples' faith was stretched to the point of breaking. But it was only as their faith, or lack of faith, was exposed that a new kind of faith emerged. Deeper. Stronger. More anchored in who God really is and in what he was doing.

And so we invite you to ask the hard questions. Pull the weeds of doubt that are strangling your joy and your peace and hope. Confess any sin that has you entangled, blinded, and distracted by what is temporary. What is fleeting. What will not survive. The stuff that has no home in eternity. We invite you to cling to God instead, preaching to yourself and to your heart what is true, what will last, what will sustain you: words and promises and songs of God's power, faithfulness, and goodness.

God's goodness not just to others, but to you.

> Taste and see that the Lord is good;
> blessed is the one who takes refuge in him.
> Fear the Lord, you his holy people,
> for those who fear him lack nothing.
> The lions may grow weak and hungry,
> but those who seek the Lord lack no good thing. . . .
> The righteous cry out, and the Lord hears them;
> he delivers them from all their troubles.
> The Lord is close to the brokenhearted
> and saves those who are crushed in spirit. (Ps. 34:8–10, 17–18)

As hard as it may be right now, Jesus is asking us too, "Do you still have no faith?" Jesus is asking us to trust him and have faith that what he has done for others, he can and wants to do for us too.

HELP ME OVERCOME MY LITTLE FAITH

Several nights after we heard the word "cancer" for the first time, about twenty of our closest friends and members of our church gathered in a home. They prayed. Worshipped. And one by one, they read God's Word over Patrick. Soaking him, if you will, and surrounding him with God's truth.

One friend shared the story of a father whose son was sick. It's a story from Mark's gospel as well. A few chapters after the storm the disciples were in.

The boy, as the father told Jesus, had been suffering since he was just a child under the influence of spiritual attacks. When the impure spirit would come upon the boy, the spirit would gnash his teeth, foam at the mouth, and even throw the boy into fire or water. You can imagine the father's concern, fear, and helplessness.

The disciples could do nothing about it, we're told. And so the man brought his heavy heart to the One he knew could do something. Anything.

The father pled with Jesus, "But if you can do anything, take pity on us and help us" (Mark 9:22).

This is perhaps one of the best pictures of prayer—bringing our helplessness and neediness to Jesus. This, in and of itself, is an act of faith.

"'If you can?' said Jesus. 'Everything is possible for one who believes'" (Mark 9:23).

And then, one verse later, the father humbly confessed, "I do believe; help me overcome my unbelief!"

When our friend read that story and that passage, it hit close to home for us. Suffering reveals what we really believe. The parts of our hearts that don't yet believe. And like the father in Mark's story, we do believe. We want to believe. Yet we need God's grace to believe and keep believing.

We need to admit where we are and ask God for more grace to help us overcome our unbelief. The goodness of God, as seen in this story, is that Jesus healed the boy. Came through anyway. Restored and set free. Even with the father's little faith struggling to overcome unbelief.

We often feel that way. Suffering has revealed what we do believe, the places where our faith is strong and secure. But it has also revealed where we still need more of God's grace, the places where we are asking Jesus to "help our unbelief."

We need to "take up the shield of faith," fighting fear and doubt and lies from the Enemy (Eph. 6:16). Because, ultimately, faith is not about us. It's about who God is. It's about what God is capable of.

Our faith might waver, but God's faithfulness never does.

Our faith might waver, but God's faithfulness never does.

Out here on the water, in a boat, is where we usually find out we are not as strong as we think we are. What we believe gets tested. This sometimes reveals that there are places in our hearts where we don't yet believe God. Or trust him. Or think he is reliable, dependable, even good.

But it's out here in the water where we also find out God is far stronger than we think he is. Stronger than our weakness. We discover that he not only loves others but he loves us. We find out he is more faithful than our faithlessness. And we discover, like the father who said he believes, that we still need God's grace to overcome our unbelief.

Maybe that's you. It was us. And it still can be us at times. We believe. But we keep saying, "Give us more. Give us your grace. One more day, sometimes one more minute. Give us what is lacking in us. Make us whole. Help us, too, Jesus. Overcome the places in our hearts where there is *still* unbelief."

QUESTIONS FOR FURTHER REFLECTION AND DISCUSSION

1. As you think about the disciples in Mark 4, how did the storm reveal a greater threat going on inside of them?
2. How did their storm expose their faith?
3. In what ways has your suffering helped you see what you believe or don't believe?

4. Why is it tempting for you to believe in God's goodness and love for others, but not for you?
5. Where do you need Jesus to help you "overcome your unbelief?"

CHAPTER 9

WHAT SUFFERING SAVES US FROM

If you have ever tried to play Frisbee with a four-year-old, you know it's like forecasting the weather: a bit unpredictable. One throw to the right, off the house. One to the left, over the fence into the neighbors' yard. And, occasionally, one on the money.

So when Tyler, our oldest son, who at the time was only four, launched a Frisbee toward us from one end of the backyard to the other, it was anyone's guess where it would land.

This time, it landed in our rose bushes.

The problem wasn't so much where it landed; the problem was that Tyler ran after it—unaware of the thorns he was about to run into. Anticipating what was about to happen, I (Patrick) launched into motion.

I reached the rose bush just as Tyler was arriving. Stretching out my arm, I bumped him back and over but kept him out of the overgrown, thorny bushes. An accomplishment, I admit, I am still a little proud of today.

But Tyler didn't feel that way. At the time, he couldn't see the pain he was about to encounter, only the pain he was experiencing. And he didn't like it.

He had no idea what I was saving him from. And the truth is, there are probably a lot of those type of "dad arms" in our lives that we are completely unaware of until we get to heaven. For all that does go wrong in a fallen world, there is much that doesn't. There is much we are unknowingly protected from.

But here is the paradox. The thing that makes you kind of scratch your head. I was protecting my son from pain. I was holding him back from the thorns. Is it possible that sometimes God uses thorns not to hurt us but to protect us from something even more serious? Can God use suffering not as punishment but as a way to protect us?

THE PARADOX OF SUFFERING TO PROTECT US

A woman we know, who had experienced numerous miscarriages, interpreted her suffering as punishment. It was a payback of sorts. A way of righting the wrongs from her past. But we will remind you of what we reminded her: God doesn't operate that way.

Jesus was the perfect sacrifice on the cross. He suffered for us. In place of us. And so whatever the cause of the pain we are experiencing, we can be certain that it's not punishment. There is no condemnation (Rom. 8:1–4) for those who have put their faith in the finished and sufficient work of Jesus.

But there can be correction. Or maybe a better word is training. We'll come back to that in a moment. For now, it's helpful to see that God can and does use our suffering or hardship, painful as it may be, to protect us.

That's what it appears is happening in 2 Corinthians 12. And it is exactly how the apostle Paul viewed his suffering—his thorn, he called it.

There was plenty that the apostle Paul could have boasted about. He'd experienced visions and revelations from God. As one sent out from Jesus, he had a unique position of authority in the early church's foundation and formation. And yet, at some point in his life and ministry, he experienced choppy water. It came in the form of what he called a "thorn in my flesh": "Therefore, in order to keep me from becoming conceited, I was given a thorn in my flesh, a messenger of Satan, to torment me" (2 Cor. 12:7).

Nobody knows for sure what Paul's thorn was. This hasn't stopped commentators from speculating. You name it, someone has guessed it. Maybe Paul's thorn was his past struggles coming back to haunt him. A reoccurring temptation that he thought he should have conquered. Persecution. Bad eyesight. Or some other physical ailment that weakened him. Whatever it was, it was some kind of suffering. It was a painful trial. And he prayed a lot for God to take it away.

The problem was that God didn't take it away. He didn't heal Paul. He didn't get him out of the storm right away. Instead, God used it. Again, we are not saying God is punishing you. Or that suffering is good. Or that God is cruel and causes suffering. We're only saying that he can use it, turn it on its head, and actually use it for good.

Three times Paul prayed for God to deliver him. Get him out of the water back to shore. And, apparently, three times God said no.

Everyone has a thorn. Some kind of suffering that has left them feeling weak and overwhelmed. Paul doesn't say what his was, and maybe that is good. We might not know what Paul's thorn was that he prayed for God to take away. But we know with certainty what ours is.

For some of us it's a financial situation that seems impossible to overcome. For others, it might be a job or task that seems overwhelming. It could be health or physical circumstances that limit us. Maybe it's a marriage gone bad or parenting woes.

Suffering wears many hats.

What Paul found was that, instead of taking his weakness away, God transformed it. It was in his weakness, in his suffering, that he found a new strength. A stronger strength, if you will. God's abiding presence and power, which is our only hope in suffering. This is why we all find ourselves praying often, "God, give us grace. Help us. Give us more power to take another step."

Paul's pleading was met with the promise that God's grace, his life-giving power, was enough. "Three times I pleaded with the Lord to take it away from me. But he said, 'My grace is sufficient for you, for my power is made perfect in weakness'" (2 Cor. 12:8–9). And so, for Paul, there was a shift in his perspective—his focus became more on God's grace and less on his suffering. A shift, we admittedly know, takes time.

But there is something more. God was actually using physical weakness or some form of suffering to save Paul from spiritual sickness. Namely pride (v. 7). In order to protect Paul's heart from pride, we know God said no about taking his thorn away.

The thorn was the instrument of transformation. The suffering was the sanctifier.

There's the paradox. And depending on your suffering, we know it might be hard to see or comprehend, let alone appreciate right now, and that's okay. By God's grace, he'll get us there. He'll help us see what we need to see when we need to see it. But stick with us.

It seems that suffering and trials can be a place where

God is actually saving us from the more serious sickness of our own sin that can so easily hide when we are on the shore. Now Paul didn't say his thorn is the result of sin. He clearly recognized that his thorn, or whatever form of suffering he was encountering, was working to protect him from sin.

It would seem that the pain of suffering is not a form of punishment but rather one of the ways God can protect us. J. I. Packer makes this point and, commenting further, he writes, "The worst diseases are those of the spirit—pride, conceit, arrogance, bitterness, self-seeking. They are far more damaging than physical malfunction."[1]

How does God use suffering to protect us?

Suffering is not a form of punishment but rather one of the ways God can protect us.

Suffering can protect us from *bitterness*, making us more willing to forgive and extend grace. In light of what we are going through, the offense now seems so small and insignificant. So we're softer. Quicker to forgive. And slower to get angry.

Suffering can protect us from *apathy*, making us alive to our need for God. In our comfort or affluence, there was little need for God. We got along just fine. But now, suffering has awakened us to reality: the reality that we all need God, in this life and certainly in the life to come.

Suffering can protect us from *selfish ambition*, creating in us a sincere desire to love and serve others. Our trials can humble us, shaking the fragile foundations of our pride and arrogance and teaching us how small we really are. They cultivate in us a heart that seeks to honor God and let him get the recognition.

Suffering can protect us from *the sneakiness of greed.* The loss of money or material security can make us live more simply. We might still have money, but money no longer has us. The storm teaches us that it is not only futile to love money too much but also to trust money too much.

So when God doesn't take the storm away—when he doesn't remove the thorn—we can be sure that God is working in our suffering. He is never wasting it, instead working to protect us from a far deadlier disease: our spiritual sickness.

WHEN GOD'S LOVE IS GOOD, BUT NOT GENTLE

We told you we'd come back to God's discipline. So here it is: sometimes God disciplines to deal with the sin in us. Now again, this is different than saying God is punishing you for your sins. He is not. God's discipline is always out of his care, as one who loves and is deeply committed to training, preparing, and maturing his son or daughter.

God loves us too much to leave us as we are. And sometimes his love for us includes discipline. Like a good father, he is working for our good. God's love is always good but not always gentle.

Few things in life are as daunting (and, of course, enjoyable) as parenting. And few things in parenting are as challenging or heartbreaking as discipline. No parent in their right mind, or with a good heart, enjoys discipline, even when it is necessary!

We've never had a child say to us, "Thank you, Mom and Dad. I really appreciate your correction and training. I needed that rebuke. I think in the long run those consequences are more than appropriate. They will serve me well as I continue to grow and mature."

That just doesn't happen. Ever.

If we are honest, we're not all that different when we are on the receiving end of discipline—*God's discipline.*

Writing to a group of Christians enduring hardship and suffering, the writer of Hebrews reminded them, and us, that God is a Father who, out of love, disciplines his kids.

> Endure hardship as discipline; God is treating you as his children. . . . Moreover, we have all had human fathers who disciplined us and we respected them for it. How much more should we submit to the Father of spirits and live! They disciplined us for a little while as they thought best; but God disciplines us for our good, in order that we may share in his holiness. (Heb. 12:7, 9–10)

Not all of our suffering or hardship is because of sin. We often suffer or endure trials because of someone else's sin against us. We also experience pain because we live in a fallen world. Hardships are sometimes the result of spiritual attacks. And some suffering is just mysterious, like Job's. We never get an answer.

But some of our trials God is using for our training. God can, and does, use discipline to correct us, shape us, and save us. While not all of our suffering is because of sin, some of it is. Not someone else's sin, but our own. Unwise decisions, bad habits, immaturity—just to name a few! In Christ, God is our Father, and we are his sons and daughters. And out of love, he disciplines us. He is training and correcting us, so that we might grow up and experience the life he wants to give us. He wants us to "share in his holiness."

This seems to be what the psalmist had in mind when he wrote, "Before I was afflicted I went astray, but now I obey your word" (Ps.119:67). And then just a few verses later, he said, "It was good for me to be afflicted so that I might learn your decrees" (v. 71).

We must be careful to not just endure or try to quickly escape our suffering. Instead, we need to allow God's discipline to open our eyes and soften our hearts to parts of who we are that need change. That need God's grace and truth.

• • •

I (Ruth) have always prided myself on my ability to handle and carry a lot. I am an achiever. I can be self-reliant. So much so that it is easy for me to rely on my own strength rather than God's. Or other people's.

But there is no humanly possible way to shoulder the weight of both a sick spouse and children who are undoubtedly struggling to understand it all—plus my own emotional upheaval. Over the past year it quickly became obvious that I needed to change. My heart needed to change. Pride can keep us too private, maybe too independent. I've spent my life carrying more than I needed to, and it took something tragic like my husband's cancer diagnosis for me to once and for all give everything over to God and let others in.

One prayer we pray often and have found helpful is taken from Psalm 139:23–24. It is simply to ask God to "search" us. Why? So that we might "see if there is any offensive way" in us. Sin is dangerous, which is why the psalmist wanted God to search for it and root it out from his heart. But denying our sin is even more dangerous. When we deny our sin, we are really rejecting the cure—God's grace and forgiveness.

One of the gifts God gives us in our suffering is the gift of seeing who we really are. The layers get pulled back. Our eyes are opened and our hearts are exposed. That's what happened to the disciples. They not only discovered who Jesus was but also who they were.

Sometimes this discovery can feel a little discouraging!

There are all sorts of ways that we deal with who we really are, aren't there?

We can *pretend*. So we work hard to maintain an image. Look a certain way. Keep people at a distance so they don't figure out who we really are. We share only what benefits us and makes us look good. All in an effort to keep up an appearance of having it together.

We can *blame*. It's always someone else's fault, never ours. We blame it on a friend or set of circumstances. Anything to keep the blame from us. We never own our part or the sin we bring to the table.

We can *minimize*, acting like our sin isn't that big of a deal. My sin isn't that bad, is it?

And, of course, we can *defend* our sin. Put the blame on someone or something else. We get defensive when confronted and explain everything away.

We can be so good at handling sin the wrong way that we fall short of the life God wants to give when we allow him to uproot it. The writer of Hebrews said, "Let us throw off everything that hinders and the sin that so easily entangles. And let us run with perseverance the race marked out for us, fixing our eyes on Jesus, the pioneer and perfecter of faith" (Heb. 12:1–2).

Jesus is interested in perfecting our faith, in finishing the work he started. This is a journey that we have to be willing to cooperate in by first being honest about who we really are.

But where there is confession there is always God's

We need to be careful not to miss a future harvest because we are unwilling to endure a current hardship.

comfort. Second Corinthians 7:10 says, "Godly sorrow brings repentance that leads to salvation and leaves no regret." There is no condemnation (Rom. 8:1). Only life and freedom and sharing in God's holiness.

There is a "harvest" if we don't give up or give in during difficult times when we sense we are being "trained" or disciplined by God. Which is why we are often commanded to be patient in suffering (James 5:7). We need to be careful not to miss a future harvest because we are unwilling to endure a current hardship.

If God is disciplining you, be encouraged. He considers you his son or daughter. His discipline is out of love. He is remaking you and growing you. Don't give up or grow discouraged. Repent where necessary. Run to the cross. Rely on the Holy Spirit. And remember that God's love is always good, even when it is not gentle.

WHAT IS YOUR PROGNOSIS?

You don't have to be battling cancer to appreciate the relief of getting a different report. Better news. A good prognosis. Praise God we've heard the word "remission." But we haven't heard "cure" yet. There is currently no trace of cancer in my (Patrick's) body. But there's always the possibility the cancer could come back. So we rejoice over God's goodness and kindness, and we hope and pray that maybe one day we'll hear "cured" too.

And yet, in each of our storms, there is a deeper need we all have. Our greatest need is not to hear that your cancer is cured, there is a heartbeat, you got the job, your brother is going to make it, or any other announcement of good news. We need more than to just get through the storm and to the shore. There is something else going on in our boat in the middle of our lake.

One of our daily rhythms is getting up early and making coffee. We covet that alone time. Time with one another. Especially time with God. Ruth has her favorite spot on the couch. And I have mine, in a comfy mustard-colored armchair a friend gave me before I started treatment.

We dive into our Bibles. Write in our journals. Drink our coffee. Drink more coffee. And we do it all in near silence for fear of waking the kids up too early! We love them, but we also love our quiet time.

One morning we began talking about Paul's words in Romans 6:18: "You have been set free from sin." It was nothing new—a familiar verse, to be sure. We'd just studied through the book of Romans at our church. But this side of cancer, it meant something more. Something deeper.

Ruth and I talked about that dreaded "C" word—cancer.

We couldn't help but be reminded of how unmoved, how undisturbed we often are by our greater sickness: our own sin. We hope someday we hear the doctor say, "You are cured!" But, more importantly, we have the assurance of God's Word that we have been "set free from sin." We are no longer slaves to sin. Instead, a new power, a new life, the life of God, is at work in us. As serious as cancer is, sin is far more serious.

And Jesus has cured it.

Because of Jesus, we are no longer guilty before God. We are at peace with him. In a relationship that can't be severed by anything in life or death.

And yet there is this other truth or other side of the truth. We are *being* set free. We are in process. The work of God's Spirit is ongoing. It's a process that takes time and testing. Even some thorns. And deep water.

The Bible talks about this on two fronts: we already have been set free and we are being set free. In Christ we are holy, set apart, and set free to live for God. And yet we are called to become holy, set apart, and set free to live more fully for God. We are called to grow into what is already true of us.

We have an eternal life before us. But we also have a new life, a deeper life, rooted in God's grace and love and truth and power. Abundant life. A life God wants to give us now before we die and a life that will continue after we die.

God wants life for us. More life. And, oddly, suffering offers us just that.

QUESTIONS FOR FURTHER REFLECTION AND DISCUSSION

1. According to 2 Corinthians 12:7, what did the apostle Paul's suffering save him from?
2. How have you seen your storms protect you?
3. What does God promise us according to 2 Corinthians 12:8–9?
4. In what ways can we bring God and his grace into our everyday lives?
5. Are there particular areas of your own life that you believe God might be training you through or disciplining you in? Why?

CHAPTER 10

WE NEED ONE ANOTHER

"You need to call Michael."

That was my (Ruth's) advice for Patrick. Actually, it was more of an assignment. Call him or else!

Michael and his wife, Barb, are dear friends who live about three hours away in Ohio. Many years ago Michael was Patrick's youth pastor. They are one of the families who have shaped us the most, a family we deeply love and respect who has been there in our suffering. And a family who has been through their own suffering too.

Seventeen years ago, Michael was diagnosed with throat cancer. In his early thirties at the time, he did not receive a good prognosis. There was no rhyme or reason for his cancer. No one was hopeful for him.

But today, by God's grace, he is alive, doing well, and cancer-free!

I (Patrick) have learned by now that when Ruth tells me to do something, it is wise to do it. And so I called Michael. I knew I needed to because I was struggling. We were struggling. It was just a few months after the second transplant. On every level, we felt spent. Scared. Overwhelmed. Even alone. And we knew we couldn't isolate ourselves or try to gut it out on our own, which is tempting in trials.

When I owned up to how we were feeling, Michael said, "I'll be up. Pick a day that works. I am driving up and buying you lunch."

I can tell you exactly where we sat that day in Panera. The table, which location, what I ate. The details of our three hours together over lunch and in the car are crystal clear. We didn't do anything spectacular that afternoon. Except be together. And maybe that's exactly what we need most.

Togetherness.

What we need most in our suffering is the gift of someone else's presence. Not for what they do *for* us, but who they are *with* us.

If we believe that Jesus lives in us through the Spirit, then the presence of one another is the presence of Christ. Uniquely expressed through our personalities and experiences and gifts, but still the presence of Christ. This is a gift we give and receive when we choose to love and be loved.

For all of the things Job's friends did or said wrong, they got this right when Job found himself in water. The opening chapter of Job tells us that Job had it all. He was wealthy, had a large family, was upright, and feared the Lord. Things were good. And then all of that changed—in one day. Like most suffering, it came quickly. He lost it all and all seemed lost.

So when Job's friends saw him, they could barely believe their eyes. His suffering was so great that Job didn't look like Job. The writer recorded it this way:

> When Job's three friends, Eliphaz the Temanite, Bildad the Shuhite and Zophar the Naamathite, heard about all the troubles that had come upon him, they set out from their homes and met together by agreement to go and sympathize with him and comfort him. When they saw him from a distance, they could hardly recognize him; they began to weep aloud, and they tore their robes and sprinkled dust on their heads. Then they sat on the ground with him for seven days and seven nights. No one said a word to him, because they saw how great his suffering was. (Job 2:11–13)

The scriptures tell us that Job's friends wept with him. They tore their clothes. Sprinkled dust on their heads. In other words, they entered into Job's suffering with him. His suffering was *their* suffering.

For seven days and seven nights, they sat with him.

Painful, yes, but present. And no one said a word. His suffering was so great that their words wouldn't do. Their presence was enough.

Even today, among the Jewish people, this practice continues through a tradition called sitting *shiva*. *Shiva* is the Hebrew word for seven. After the burial of a loved one, the one mourning returns home for seven days to grieve. Of course, this is just the beginning. For seven days the mourner sits on a lower seat or stool, as do those who come to visit. And those who sit with the mourner are encouraged not to speak until spoken to and instead to wait. Mourn side by side. Resist trying to be helpful or insightful or even encouraging.

Instead, to first be present.

It's a reminder we all need, whether we are the ones suffering or trying to love someone else in their loss. In a day when it is so easy to send a text or "like" a social media post, what we need most is presence. We need to come close and be together.

It's what God did for us in the incarnation. He "took on flesh" (Heb. 2:14 THE MESSAGE) and dwelled among us in Christ. He came close. In love, he lowered himself to be near us and with us and for us. "The Word became flesh and made his dwelling among us. We have seen his glory, the glory of the one and only Son, who came from the Father, full of grace and truth" (John 1:14).

We need Jesus among us. And we need Jesus near us through the presence of friends who love us enough to be present in our pain. This is what real love does. Or as *The Book of the Poor in Spirit* states, "Love makes others' suffering its own."[1]

It doesn't mean we let everyone in. But we have to let someone in. With wisdom and boundaries, we have to allow those friends we trust and know and believe to be for us to get close to us.

Friends *call us out of living in our heads*, where we think about our suffering and not just feel our suffering. The place we worry and fear and fret. The place where the confusion and chaos try to control us.

Friends *speak truth*. Words of encouragement. They remind us of what God has said, what he has done, and what he has promised. They call us back to reality, ultimate reality, even when our reality includes suffering.

Friends *spur us on*. They keep us from giving up and protect us from discouragement or despair.

Friends *keep caring* even when the crisis is over. Long after people's lives return to normal and yours doesn't, friends stay in it and stick with you. And let you know you are not forgotten.

But, most importantly, friends *show up*. They are present. Because love doesn't let someone be alone too long. Which is what Michael did for me that day and what so many have done for our family. When we are hurting, we need the presence of others who know us and who will sit with us, weep with us, and be with us as we move toward healing.

CREATED FOR COMMUNITY

We've been in ministry long enough to have seen just about everything. And perhaps one of the things we've seen the most, that on the surface seems innocent, is the tendency for people to pull away in their pain. Pull away from people.

We've seen job losses. Messy divorces. Sickness. Tragic deaths. With each loss comes a decision: to choose community. Countless times we've witnessed an individual or couple decide to drift. Sometimes it was sudden, but usually it's gradual. A slow fade.

Someone slowly stops showing up at church. They miss a week, then two, then disappear entirely from their small group or Bible study. We're not saying there is never a time to be alone, to take a break, or to focus on your own soul care. There is, but it's never at the expense of pulling out of the community we so desperately need and are created for.

One of the sneakiest temptations in suffering is to feel sorry for ourselves. To feel like we are the only ones suffering. To think no one understands us or can help us. And sometimes it's not that we feel sorry for ourselves or think that no one understands us. It's just that suffering feels so overwhelming. So paralyzing.

And so we isolate ourselves because we think it just would be easier to go it alone. Gut it out. This is both unwise and dangerous! It's why the writer of Proverbs said "Whoever isolates himself seeks his own desire; he breaks out against all sound judgment" (Prov. 18:1 ESV).

Suffering is not just what *I* do or what *you* do; it's what *we* do. We need one another to make it.

While everyone's suffering is unique, suffering is never something we should do alone. That's certainly not what Jesus intended. When Jesus called those first disciples, he called them as individuals. But he also called them into community. Into relationship. Into a new family.

That's what the good news of God's love does. It births us into a new family. We have a new Father, new brothers and sisters, a new purpose, a new future, and a new identity.

It's why one of the things Jesus said about family was so radical. Out of the ordinary and countercultural. Jesus redefined family. Family isn't biological; it's theological. One chapter before the disciples found themselves in a boat, they found themselves in a house. They were listening to Jesus teach when his family showed up. Mark recorded the story this way:

Suffering is not just what *I* do or what *you* do; it's what *we* do. We need one another to make it.

> Then Jesus' mother and brothers arrived. Standing outside, they sent someone in to call him. A crowd was sitting around him, and they told him, "Your mother and brothers are outside looking for you."
>
> "Who are my mother and my brothers?" he asked.

> Then he looked at those seated in a circle around him and said, "Here are my mother and my brothers! Whoever does God's will is my brother and sister and mother." (Mark 3:31–35)

Those were explosive words in Jesus' day! Following Jesus costs a lot. To follow Jesus often meant to give up one's family of origin, one's biological family. But it also meant gaining a new family by becoming part of God's family, the church.

The church is described in a lot of ways in the New Testament. But the picture most often used is that of a family. A lesson the disciples were beginning to learn that day was that they weren't just disciples; they were family.

Each of us are being discipled by Jesus. But as brothers and sisters who are family, we are also discipling one another.

We are loving one another. Serving one another. Giving sacrificially to one another. Carrying one another's burdens. Forgiving one another. Praying for one another. Speaking truth to one another. And, all along the way, we are helping one another grow up into the fullness of who God wants us to be—like Jesus.

All of this is only possible when we choose community. When we stay in the family and stay connected to a local church.

What does this have to do with suffering? A lot.

When it comes to suffering and water and storms, we are called into the waves together. Called to walk through it with and for one another. This was certainly the case when Jesus first told the disciples to lay down their nets and follow him. And it was true out on the water when he said, "Let us go over to the other side."

Note the "us."

We all suffer. But we aren't meant to suffer alone. We need one another. Ecclesiastes 4:10 tells us, "If one person falls, the other can reach out and help. But someone who falls alone is in real trouble" (NLT).

Sometimes that love we need comes to us. But often we have to choose that love and give people permission to love us. We have to let people in. Ask for help. Or call a friend.

We were created for community, but most often we have to choose community.

BE CAREFUL OF BEING HURT IN YOUR HURT

"I felt forgotten," a woman told us not long after she lost her daughter. The community she had chosen and the one she was created for crumbled. We didn't know all of her circumstances or whether she had really been forgotten or not. She lived in a different city and attended a different church.

But it didn't matter. Her pain was still pain. Loss is loss no matter where you live.

She described the different ways people responded to her suffering. "At first," she told us, "it was overwhelmingly good. Almost too much. They loved on us by calling and stopping by. Our church brought us meals and prayed for us regularly. They took our other kids to the movies."

As time moved on, though, and the trial faded, so did people's questions and interest. "People stopped asking. It felt like everyone moved on except us," she said.

No matter the circumstances, her story reveals a temptation we can all face in our suffering. The temptation to be hurt in our hurt.

After the last few years of facing cancer, we can certainly appreciate all the different ways people respond to our hurt. Even with the many people who respond graciously, there are the moments our hearts can feel overlooked, not cared for, and still wanting for more in our relationships. Like all pain, it hurts. And what we'll see is that it's another way God is drawing us closer to his love.

Not everyone responds to suffering in the same way. A woman recently asked us how things were going. "Give me an update," she said. So we did.

By the look on her face you would have thought a small animal was lodged in her loafer, gnawing away at her big toe. She winced. Grimaced. And contorted her face in such a way that, by the time we were done giving her a positive update, we wondered if we should be worried! It was clear that her response, like that of many, was fear. Because, after all, if a pastor can get cancer, can't anyone?

So many people responded with sympathy and support. We received cards and letters. Gift cards to local restaurants. Countless texts and messages. We had friends clean our home, mow our yard, take care of our kids, pray for us, and visit us. There is nothing like the church. The church is an incredible family that took care of us beautifully.

And then there were some who responded with silence. This is a suffering in and of itself. People we love and had been close to didn't reach out. They didn't call. Or text. No visits. Those we thought would love us left us in our suffering.

This was perhaps one of the biggest surprises, one of the unexpected pieces of our heart that we would have to reckon with. What do we do with this?

The writer of Proverbs said it this way: "One who has unreliable friends soon comes to ruin, but there is a friend who sticks closer than a brother" (Prov. 18:24).

There are some, the writer said, who are "unreliable." We suspect there are a lot of ways to be unreliable, but at the very least, it refers to people who we thought would be there for us but turned out not to be. They ran away from our suffering instead of running toward it. But there are some who through suffering and storms and trials prove to be like family. They stick close. Stay committed. Run to us. Sit with us. Stay in it. As long as it takes.

So what about those who don't? We're learning that this, too, is part of the process and the way God meets us. Remakes us and shapes us and transforms us. Pulling us closer. Drawing us deeper.

But the temptation is there—to be hurt in our hurt. We have to be watchful and guard our hearts from these kinds of hurts. Why? Because, as good as friends are, as necessary as community is, it can never be enough for the dark places. The deepest hurt that only God can meet us in.

We're learning that even the best of friends cannot love us like God does.

Jesus knew this and even modeled it for us. In his time of greatest need, he experienced both the joy of community and the hurt of community. When he was telling his disciples about his suffering, about the cross, he told them that they wouldn't stick around. There would be a time when it would be too much. He knew they would leave him, but even when they did, he would not be alone.

> A time is coming and in fact has come when you will be scattered, each to your own home. You will leave me all alone. Yet I am not alone, for my Father is with me. I have told you these things, so that in me you may have peace. In this world you will have trouble. But take heart! I have overcome the world. (John 16:32–33)

It's true; we desperately need the presence of others. And yet Jesus is reminding us that community only takes us so far. It can only do so much.

Our closest friends can support us but never truly satisfy us. Our deepest need for love and support and understanding can only be met in the love of our Father, through Jesus, and in the powerful presence of the Holy Spirit. We can't expect friends to do what only our Father can do. We have to be careful of having unrealistic expectations or desiring our friends to meet all of our needs. They can't. They won't. They weren't meant to.

Resist feeling hurt in our hurt. We need to love anyway. For isn't this what Jesus did? And isn't this moving closer to what real love is? The kind Jesus poured out—a selfless and sacrificial love?

We know in your hurt you might not be there yet. Many days we're not either. But we are convinced that God meets us in this place to love us and fill us and satisfy us like no one else can.

YOUR BEST NEXT STEP?

How should you approach relationships and community in this season?

For us, it was time to open up. Invite someone in. Call a friend. But it was also time to let friends support us without expecting them to satisfy us, which requires seeing that our deepest longings can only be met in a God who loves us unconditionally and is with us in the storm. God knows exactly what we are going through. When we feel like no one understands, we know Jesus does, because he suffered for us.

What is the right next step for you?

Maybe it's time to admit you are hurting. Set aside your pride. Crucify the image of having it all together. Or perhaps you need to forgive and ask God for the grace to love those you feel haven't loved you the way you needed or wanted.

We know it's not easy to let others in. It's not always comfortable to allow people to feel your tears, hear your fears, or see your weaknesses.

But it's worth it.

We have friends who would gladly dig through a roof for us (Mark 2). They have carried us on our stretcher. They have placed us at the feet of Jesus. Over and over again. Friends have loved us, sacrificed for us, cried with us, and prayed for us.

Love never lets someone be alone for too long.

Love never lets someone be alone for too long. Let those around you love you. It's one of the ways God meets us in our chaos. He meets us out on the water in the storm. He meets us through the friends who love us the most.

QUESTIONS FOR FURTHER REFLECTION AND DISCUSSION

1. Why are we often tempted to isolate ourselves when we are hurting? How can this be good but also dangerous?
2. How have you been tempted to withdraw from community?
3. What is one way you can cultivate deeper friendship in your suffering?
4. In what ways are you at risk of being hurt in your hurt?
5. Why is it crucial to remember that friends can support us but never ultimately satisfy us like God can?

CHAPTER 11

YOU HAVE A FUTURE

We had been living in Bryan, Ohio, for only about a year when we decided to take a drive to Toledo, Ohio, a city we had lived in for nearly ten years. We wanted to see our old house.

We had brought each of our kids home to that house. It was nothing fancy. Built in 1903, it came with lots of character, but it needed a lot of care. It was desperately in need of painting. The windows were drafty and brittle. Pieces of the kitchen floor were missing, worn out by time and beat up by traffic. But it was home.

Home is never just about the place, though, is it? It's about the people who live there.

For ten years, it was ours. As a family. And now someone else lived there. A year earlier we had sold it. Moved to a new town. Settled into a new house. This new house was an hour from Fort Wayne, Indiana, where I (Patrick) was born and raised. Two hours from where Ruth grew up. And only an hour from the house we started our family in.

As we jostled back and forth, visiting different places we had called home, something happened in us. We began to notice that nowhere felt like home anymore. Of course, parts of each of those places did and still do. But we noticed that it was the first time we felt a little homesick. Each of those homes represented times and people and places we could never get back to if we wanted to.

A new longing began to emerge in us. Home, it seemed, was no longer behind us. Or even where we were at currently. Home, or the feeling of being at home, began to feel like it was ahead of us.

And, as it turns out, this theme of home and homesickness is God-given. It's where we want to end our book, because, ultimately, home is what we're all looking for. It's where we are all heading. It's where all the hurting will stop and the joy and belonging and goodness will begin. It's where the rest and reunion will happen.

As we'll see, the discovery of feeling "out of place" is one more way God meets us in our chaos. It's one more way he reminds us, home is before us and not just behind us. The storm has another side that we'll get to, even if we have to endure the choppy waters first.

As we look at Mark 4 one last time, there is one

more detail we need to take notice of. One more important truth. Remember that before the storm hit, Jesus had promised his disciples that they would make it to the other side. "Let us go over to the other side," he said (Mark 4:35).

And then the storm hit.

We're guessing the disciples discovered a new desire to reach the shore once they were in the storm. It wasn't until the water surrounded them and the waves threatened to engulf them that the longing began to grow in them, more than when they first set out. Which is what suffering always does. It wakes us up to a deeper longing for safe arrival. For a new destination. One that the Bible describes as heaven. But, as we'll see, that is only part of the promise.

Just as Jesus promised those first disciples safe arrival on the "other side," we have the promise of a new future. A better future.

Jesus has a future for you. It might be a new marriage. Better health. Another child. More money. He wants good for you. But most importantly, we have a future with God. Whether in life or death, we belong to God, the scriptures promise (Rom. 14:8). And it will feel like coming home, to the place and people we have always longed for.

God might not take away our homesickness, but right now, in the middle of our weeping, he wants to transform it—giving us hope, even joy, when it hurts. Our hope is transforming our hurt as we look forward to God's return.

Hope isn't just something *we* hold on to in the dark; hope holds *us* when we feel surrounded by the dark.

And what we are noticing in our own hearts is a new longing. Something God wants for us. And something he gives to us when he meets us in our chaos. A longing for home. For heaven. Frederick Buechner, in agreement with his mentor, Dr. Buttrick, said that "the home we long for and belong to is finally where Christ is."[1]

Hope isn't just something *we* hold on to in the dark; hope holds *us* when we feel surrounded by the dark.

Homesickness, it turns out, is something we are all born with. It's groaning and growing within us. And homesickness might tell us more about our future than we realize.

WE WERE BORN HOMESICK

The Bible begins with humanity at home. God took the stuff of earth, working it and cultivating it, building it so it was just right for Adam and Eve to live in. It was the perfect space, as the name indicated. The garden of Eden was a garden of "delight."

The eternal God, who is Father, Son, and Spirit, filled Eden with his presence. God's real estate is always relational. He was building a home where we could belong and he could belong with us.

As a good parent, God walked, talked, and dwelled with his kids. Creation was at ease. It never flinched, ached, or groaned. There was no weeping, because all was as it should be. It was what every home was meant to be. It was a place of loving relationship, joy, beauty, safety, discovery, security, and intimacy. Sadly, we didn't stay at home long. It was soon divided, splintered, and eventually lost.

Adam and Eve were not content to be at home with their Father. He had given them everything they needed. Everything they could have wanted. Except they weren't God. Anxious to leave home and explore life on their own terms, Adam's and Eve's sin to break relationship with their Father would have devastating effects on them and everyone who would follow.

Even though God had lovingly warned them not to eat from the Tree of Knowledge of Good and Evil, they thought they knew better. They hardened their hearts by closing their ears. And then they opened their mouths to eat. The Bible describes this act of rebellion and distrust in our Father's goodness when it says that the "woman saw that the fruit of the tree was good for food and pleasing to the eye, and also desirable for gaining wisdom, she took some and ate it" (Gen. 3:6). We had always envisioned Adam in a distant room or far corner. But this account tells us that Adam was right there "with her, and he ate it" too (v. 6). Feeling exposed for the first time, they tried to cover their sin. Instead of running home, they ran away. "They sewed fig leaves and made coverings for themselves" (v. 7).

Eden would be lost when God "banished" them from the garden (v. 23). The home they once lived in would now be the home they longed for. And, for the first time, humanity would know and experience the pain of feeling "out of place." Out of the womb and into the world we now come, with this sickness for home beating in our chest.

God wired us for home. And to a certain degree, our earthly homes are supposed to be miniature Edens. For many of us, home is where we first experience what it means to be loved. It's where we discover the security of belonging. Homes don't just define where we live, but in many ways, they define who we are. Which is why leaving home can be so hard. But even these homes we have to eventually leave.

So it's no surprise that we all experience homesickness in different ways and in different seasons. Eventually we leave our home, but our longing for home, the one God made us for, never leaves us. We all live with that "memory." We never outgrow homesickness.

We were not born in Eden but outside of it. And as beautiful as this life is, it's not enough. It's temporary. A prelude of sorts, of what is to come. It's why the New Testament describes us as "exiles" and "foreigners" (1 Peter 2:11).

God has made us to hunger and thirst, long and wait,

for a new home. A greater home. A restoration of what went wrong in the garden of Delight. The road to this home is bumpy. It's full of suffering and weakness and pain. But the weeping is meant to be like a welcome mat. Instead of feeling homesick for the place behind us, we begin to long for a home that is ahead of us.

In the chaos, Jesus takes our loss and turns it into longing.

LONGING FOR A NEW AND GREATER HOME

We're pretty good at eavesdropping. When out to dinner, I (Ruth) have to routinely tell Patrick, "Come back to *our* conversation!"

It's true.

I (Patrick) have had countless conversations begin because I invited myself into someone else's! At the bookstore. A game. Once at a gas station. Most recently, a coffee shop.

I heard the barista say, "Who would want to go to heaven?" Living in Ann Arbor, it's not uncommon to hear spiritual conversations. And I figured, if she was asking a question, I might as well answer it—even though, technically, she wasn't asking me.

"I mean, if heaven is floating around on a cloud, listening to angelic harpists, I'm not interested," she said.

"I'm with you," I said. If that is our future, no wonder we hold on so tightly to our past. Or present. No wonder this life is what we think about most. While we didn't solve every mystery about heaven that day in the coffee shop, I did help her see that much of what heaven will be is exactly what her heart is longing for. And different from how our culture usually pictures heaven, the Bible presents a future that is far more inviting.

We'll be the first to admit that before cancer, we didn't think too much about heaven. We didn't talk about it a lot. Read about it. Or really study it much. I had never even preached a series on it. When you are young and healthy, heaven seems like a distant thought. A home we know is ahead of us, but not one we are necessarily curious about and looking forward to.

But suffering changes all of that. You don't have to have cancer to begin to have a new perspective. A deeper awareness of the brevity of life. Just the passing of time is a persistent and unrelenting reminder of our mortality.

The psalmist said that God has been from "everlasting to everlasting" (Ps. 90:2). There was never a time when God was not. He is eternal. And yet our lives are fleeting. Like a breath that quickly appears on a cold and chilly winter morning, then disappears.

> Show me, Lord, my life's end
> and the number of my days;
> let me know how fleeting my life is.

> You have made my days a mere handbreadth;
> the span of my years is as nothing before you.
> Everyone is but a breath,
> even those who seem secure. (Ps. 39:4–5)

So if we could encourage you in any way right now, it would be to remember that your suffering is temporary. God is eternal. What he has for us is going to last forever. But it's critical that we not only think often and more about heaven but think rightly.

In the New Testament, we are encouraged to set our hearts and minds on heaven:

> Since, then, you have been raised with Christ, set your hearts on things above, where Christ is, seated at the right hand of God. Set your minds on things above, not on earthly things. For you died, and your life is now hidden with Christ in God. When Christ, who is your life, appears, then you also will appear with him in glory. (Col. 3:1–4)

To "set" our hearts on things above is to seek after heaven. To think about it. Meditate on it. Desire it. And by God's grace, we will increasingly find ourselves longing more and more for what is ours in Christ. And for Christ himself.

But again, we need to think rightly to have a clearer picture of what is to come.

A BETTER PICTURE OF HEAVEN

The barista I (Patrick) encountered is not the only one confused about heaven. It can be hard for all of us to fully wrap our minds around what God has promised. And while the Bible doesn't tell us everything about the future, it does tell us a lot. Plenty to look forward to. And plenty we should be hopeful of.

Entire books have been written on the topic, but here are just a few important truths to keep in mind that God uses to encourage us and give us hope when he meets us in our storm.

Heaven is a *physical place.* The Bible ends not with us going up to heaven, but heaven coming down to us. A rejoining of heaven and earth. God is going to renew and restore creation (2 Peter 3:13). There will be a new heaven and a new earth, no longer tainted by sin. And Jesus said it will feel like home (John 14:1–3). We will not be spirits floating around on clouds. The body is good, and just as Jesus had a resurrected and glorified body, we will as well. Why? Because a physical earth, restored and renewed, is in our future.

Heaven will *last forever.* It is permanent (2 Cor. 5:1). Eternal love. Everlasting joy. Unending security and belonging. Perfect and abiding peace. By our faith in Jesus, we have been born into a "living hope." We've been given an inheritance that will not perish, spoil, or fade. An inheritance that is kept in heaven for us (1 Peter 1:1–5).

Heaven will be a place where *we will be reunited.* Reunited to God in Christ but also reunited to loved ones. Family members and friends. It will feel like a family regathering (1 Thess. 4:17). A place where the party does not end.

Just as Adam and Eve enjoyed creation, labored, and worked, stewarding and cultivating God's good earth, we will do the same. Work will be meaningful and fruitful. We'll do something. And that something will be rewarding (Matt. 25:21).

The thing with suffering is it often feels like it is killing the future. It can feel like someone has taken a knife and severed ministry plans. Dreams for a family. Retirement together. Financial prosperity or security. Or a thousand other ideas we put on the shelf for tomorrow.

Ruth and I have always been dreamers. And when we were thrust into the world of cancer, our future felt dead. We stopped dreaming about book ideas. Vision for the church ceased. Growing old together seemed far-fetched. Today became enough to crawl through.

Our joy and hope, if it is to sustain us, can never be in how our trials turn out, but who our trials lead us to.

The good news is that, in Jesus, God would come looking for all of us lost ones (John 1:14). He'd tell stories about lost coins, lost sheep, and wayward children far from home. All the while, God would be inviting us back home—telling us the truth about the way back to life, life in him. Not only would we find our home in God, but God would make his home in us.

We don't just grow out of homesickness; a new kind of homesickness begins to grow in us. We begin to long not for an earthly home, the one we grew up in or have fond memories of, but we begin to long for eternity. We begin to long for heaven, even if heaven is full of mystery. The pain of missing our earthly home is just pointing us toward a greater home.

THE PAIN WILL BE WORTH IT

Before we get to the promise, we have to go through some pain.

I'll (Ruth) never forget the night our first son, Tyler, was born. It was 10:02 p.m. on June 29, 2002. Pre-birth I had visions of being a caring, sensitive mom, holding Patrick's hand while I pushed and he cheered me on!

And then reality hit. Labor pains began. Contractions. Sweating. Irritated glances. Six weeks of classes, in a second, thrown out the window. I wouldn't let Patrick even talk to me, let alone touch me. We were having a baby. I was having a baby. The promise of new life meant going through a whole lot of pain first.

In the New Testament book of Romans, the apostle Paul described the world as it is now like a mom reeling, sometimes thrashing, with the pain of childbirth.

"The whole creation," Paul wrote, is "groaning as in the pains of childbirth" (Rom. 8:22). Paul was describing the way things are. We are no longer in Eden. Creation is no longer at ease. Jaws clenched, we ache. We are all "groan[ing] inwardly" (v. 23). Like a hopeful mom, pushing and breathing, cursing and clenching for what is on the other side.

If that's not enough, Paul also likened us to sons and daughters waiting for our full adoption when Christ returns. As sons and daughters far from home, sometimes we feel like orphans. The cancer, loss of a job, wayward child, or miscarried baby leaves us weeping, wondering about the fatherhood of God. If not for hope, we'd stay there, convinced that the way it is must be the way it is.

But all is not as it seems. Paul told us that somewhere in the middle of the groaning, something else is growing. We "wait eagerly" as we "groan inwardly" for our homecoming. It's a long walk, but our Father has put his Spirit in us as a guarantee that the redemption, the regathering of family, is coming (Rom. 8:23). The pain will be worth it, Paul added. "For I consider that the sufferings of this present time are not worth comparing with the glory that will be revealed in us" (v. 18).

Jesus didn't come for nothing; Jesus came to make all things new.

We are in the world, but because we are in Christ, the world as it is, is fading. Eventually the hurt will be cast off. And so, Paul said, we wait patiently, eagerly looking and longing for that day when Jesus will wipe away every tear, kill death, and give us back what was lost. The writer of the very last book of the Bible described a vision God gave him of what that homecoming will look like. He wrote:

> And I heard a loud voice from the throne saying, "Look! God's dwelling place is now among the people, and he will dwell with them. They will be his people, and God himself will be with them and be their God. He will wipe every tear from their eyes. There will be no more death or mourning or crying or pain, for the old order of things has passed away." (Rev. 21:3–4)

This is the home we were made for. Through faith, Christ has made his home in us. The pain and loss we often feel from being out of place is meant to remind us that we aren't home yet. We are "aliens and strangers" (1 Peter 2:11 NASB). We live as "exiles" (1 Peter 1:1), treading lightly, even temporarily, until the permanence of the promise comes at last. We are sons and daughters who sometimes feel like orphans until we make it home. And we will make it home. Because we have a future.

There is one more detail we don't want you to miss. As the writer was describing his vision of this newly restored heaven and earth, he makes sure to tell us "there was no longer any sea" (Rev. 21:1). Many commentators would agree that this doesn't literally mean there will be no more water in heaven. It is more likely a symbolic way of saying death and evil and pain and chaos will be no more. We would add, we'll no longer be in a boat in the middle of a lake.

So what does all this mean for us? Right now? A lot. Remember what Paul said in 2 Corinthians 4:16–18 (emphasis added):

> Therefore we do not lose heart. Though outwardly we are wasting away, yet inwardly we are being renewed day by day. For our *light and momentary troubles* are achieving for us an *eternal glory* that far *outweighs them all*. So we fix our eyes not on what is seen, but on what is unseen, since what is seen is *temporary*, but what is unseen is *eternal*.

It means we should not give up. We should resist growing discouraged. "We do not lose heart." Because as heavy and scary and overwhelming as the storm may be, it won't last forever (v. 17). Our suffering has an expiration date. And our "light and momentary troubles" will be met with glory and goodness forever. In other words, it will be worth it.

We should be careful, then, of looking at the way things are (v. 18) and, instead, focus on the way things will be. Our pain. The loss. The aching and pounding. It will all disappear. It is temporary. But home, heaven, where God is, will last forever. Fix your eyes there. Set your affection on that reality.

FROM HOMESICKNESS TO A HOMECOMING

A friend of mine (Patrick) called me one day with a question we had no answer to. He had a son who, for a variety of reasons, had been confined to a wheelchair most of his life. He was turning ten in just a few days and was convinced that, when he did, he was going to be able to walk for the first time.

"What should I tell him?" my friend asked me. "Do I let him think he is going to walk on his birthday? I've prayed for years that God would heal him."

These are the kinds of calls and questions that punch you in the gut. That leave you without words.

Our friend was not only asking a question, he was groaning inwardly. His heart was aching. Longing for the hurt to stop and the weight to be lifted. We won't pretend to know what it's like for a father to watch his son roll out of bed and land on limp, buckling legs. We won't pretend to know the heaviness of seeing your son in a heap and scooping him off the floor, again. We've never felt that burden or cried those tears.

I didn't know what to say at first when he called. I wanted to reach my hand through the phone and hold his, giving him rest even for just a moment. My mind darted to the last time we wheeled my mom into the hospital. We didn't know it was the last time she, too, would be confined to her wheelchair. November in Indiana is cold enough. It's even colder when you say goodbye to the ones you love the most.

My sisters and I had put hundreds of miles on her chair. We pushed her to appointments. Helped her out of vehicles. Trekked to church. Made lots of trips to Cracker Barrel! And racked up plenty of miles around her apartment. But in the early hours of November 5, we pushed her ride to my sister's car—without her. She finally snuck home. She left behind what she wouldn't need anymore and was home to where the aching stops, the tears cease, the lame walk, the blind see, the mute speak, the deaf hear, and the groaning turns to glory.

So I told my friend the only thing I know with much certainty. That we suffer, but not without a promise. The light is on, and our Father is calling. We might not be home yet, but home is on the way. I told him to tell his son, "Keep trying." Keep trying with defiance. Keep trying until the darkness is damned. It might not be on his tenth birthday, but one of these days he's going to land on solid ground, strong legs and steady feet. He, too, will leave behind what he doesn't need.

God never fully takes away our homesickness, but eventually, through weeping, he transforms it. Hope transforms our hurt into patient waiting. Hope enables us to see through the tears to what is coming, to what we are really searching for. One of the ways God changes us

We might not be home yet, but home is on the way.

in our weeping is by helping us to long for the home that will last. The home that is not behind us but ahead of us.

At some point our feelings of homesickness turn into longing for our homecoming. We begin to accept we can't ever get back what we once had. Or maybe we come to grips that the places and people we used to associate with home are no longer there. Some places will always be home but, at the same time, stop feeling like home. God uses our weeping, suffering, and trials to teach us that home is coming.

So we do what the writer of Hebrews said. We "hold unswervingly to the hope we profess, for he who promised is faithful" (Heb. 10:23). We have not yet received all of the promises. We see them from afar, but eagerly welcome them.

We'd encourage you with the truth that your chaos has no future. Your loss will not last. The heaviness of pain will be swallowed by the promise. You have a future. And it is a future of God's goodness. A gift to you. A reward for persevering in pain.

You might be in a boat in the middle of a lake. But you are not alone. And that lake has another side. One Jesus has promised to get you to. "Let us go over to the other side," Jesus said. There will be many storms. Some smaller. And maybe some bigger. But there is a shore. We'll say it again: there is a shore.

The promise of safe arrival.

Rest.

Renewal.

Victory.

Home.

God's presence.

"Surely your goodness and love will follow me all the days of my life, and I will dwell in the house of the Lord forever" (Ps. 23:6).

So let us press on in the storm. Let's continue to trust the God who meets us in our storm.

Your chaos will cease. It will not last. You have a future. We have a future. And it's a future filled with God's goodness and love and beauty. It's a future filled with God himself.

QUESTIONS FOR FURTHER REFLECTION AND DISCUSSION

1. Take a moment and read Colossians 3:1–4. How does thinking about our future encourage us in the present?
2. What does God promise us in 1 Peter 1:1–5?
3. How does the promise of 2 Corinthians 4:16–18 help put our pain in perspective?
4. How does the feeling of homesickness lead us to experience greater hope?
5. What truth about heaven do you need to hold on to right now?

ACKNOWLEDGMENTS

Shortly after we heard the word *cancer*, I (Patrick) called my two sisters, Sara and Sandy. They were the hardest two calls to make, but also the best. Each of them showed me love and offered support in ways we'll always be grateful for.

As I was getting ready to hang up the phone, my oldest sister said to me, "all eyes are on you." What my sisters meant was that for nearly twenty years I had preached God's Word, cared for others, and led in several local churches. Many people had listened to me, but now they would be watching me walk through the most difficult season of my life.

I received similar encouragement from a friend you met in the book, Michael, a stage-four cancer survivor. I sat in my driveway and called him as well. Before hanging up he, too, reminded me that my kids would be watching us suffer.

If we could do the last two years again, there is certainly much we would change. We haven't always been a perfect witness, or always been worth watching. But early on we decided we were not going to waste our suffering.

As we mentioned in the book, we are not experts in suffering. Our motivation for writing *In a Boat in the Middle of a Lake* was to encourage others that in whatever storm they found themselves—God is trustworthy. He not only meets us in the storm, but we are deeply molded by him, in the storm. We hope that has been true in your boat. In your storm. And in whatever water you are in.

In our boat, there were many by our side and for that we are forever grateful.

First, to our own kids—Tyler, Bella, Noah, and Sophia: this has not been easy for us and we know it hasn't been easy for you. We wish you didn't have to know this pain or feel this fear. But just as with us, we know Jesus is going to use this in your life, too, for your good and God's glory. We love you and are proud of your faith and courage over the past two years. We have no greater joy than knowing that you are walking in the truth and holding on to the same hope.

To Patrick's parents: there was rarely a day that went by that I did not think about each of you—now a part of heaven's "cloud of witnesses." You went before me, and I am grateful you did. You modeled for me a life of endurance, faith, and trust. The Jesus you preached when I was a kid is the Jesus who sustained me in my cancer. And he is the same Jesus who will raise me up one day, when we see each other again.

To Ruth's parents: we could not have faced the last two years without you. You made Patrick's favorite soup countless times when he was in the hospital and then when he came home. You remodeled our basement, a project you had just started a month before his diagnosis. And of course, you made us laugh! You were a steady and stable presence for us—and for your grandkids—when everything felt like it was unraveling. Thank you for your selfless and sacrificial love.

To Patrick's sisters: this was not the first time we found ourselves "in a boat in the middle of a lake." We said goodbye to dad in 2010. And goodbye to mom in 2012. Each of you have suffered in your own unique and painful ways, before walking with me through my suffering. Whether it was coming to meet us for lunch, visiting in the hospital, texting or calling, we never felt alone in our boat in the middle of a lake. You were with us in the water. We love you and are grateful for the countless ways you cared for us and our family.

To our Refuge Church family in Ann Arbor: when I told our kids to "watch the church," you did not disappoint. You were the presence of Christ to us in hundreds of tangible ways. You cleaned our home, brought us meals, faithfully prayed, showed up to appointments, let me cry in every sermon—the list goes on! We could not have faced this without you. We moved to Ann Arbor together to start a church, but first and foremost, you were the church to us. Thank you for loving us, supporting us, and showing us grace in our hurt and our healing.

Thank you to our friends who stood with us from afar with your constant calls, texts, and prayers. Michael and Barb, Terry and Susan, Todd and Karen, Ron and Sandra, Courtney, and many more not mentioned—we are forever grateful for your friendship and love.

Thank you to the readers of *The Better Mom* and *For the Family* blogs. For so many of you, our fight was your fight. You stuck with us, not just watching from a distance but interceding for us. Words can't express our thankfulness for your many comments, messages, and prayers. We are blessed to be on this journey with each of you.

Thank you to Meredith Brock, our friend and agent. From the beginning you have been far more interested in God's message and not just a creative idea. You are a woman of God, full of faith, wisdom, and compassion. You have also been one of our biggest cheerleaders. We are so grateful for you!

Finally, to our amazing team at Nelson Books: thank you to Jessica Wong, Brigitta Nortker, Jamie Lockard, Kristen Golden, and Shea Nolan. We are so grateful for your guidance, encouragement, and confidence in this message. We are humbled and honored to work alongside you.

NOTES

Chapter 3: This *Is* What God Is Doing

1. *The Merriam-Webster Dictionary*, s.v. "interruption," accessed December 7, 2019, https://www.merriam-webster.com /dictionary/interruption.
2. St. Augustine, *Confessions*, trans. Henry Chadwick (Oxford: Oxford University Press, 2009), 3.
3. Andrew Murray, *Waiting on God*, updated ed. (Abbotsford, WI: Aneko Press, 2018), 6–7.

Chapter 4: Pry Me Off Dead Center

1. Brennan Manning, *Ruthless Trust: The Ragamuffin's Path to God* (New York: HarperOne, 2000), 2.

Chapter 7: We Are Not Alone

1. C. S. Lewis, *A Grief Observed* (New York: HarperOne, 2015), 6.
2. Mother Teresa, *Come Be My Light* (New York: Image, 2009), 1, 2.
3. C. H. Spurgeon, *Evening by Evening: Readings at Eventide*

(New York: Sheldon & Company, 1869), 318, available in Spurgeon, *Morning and Evening*, November 11, evening reading (public domain).
4. The concept of gradual spiritual maturity outlined here is found in greater detail and explanation in Janet Hagberg and Robert Guelich, *The Critical Journey: Stages in the Life of Faith* (Salem, WI: Sheffield Publishing Company, 2005).
5. Thomas Merton, *No Man Is an Island* (Boulder, CO: Shambhala Publications, 2005), 250.

Chapter 8: Discovering What We Really Believe

1. C. S. Lewis, *A Grief Observed* in *The Complete C. S. Lewis Signature Classics* (New York: HarperCollins, 2002), 448.

Chapter 9: What Suffering Saves Us From

1. J. I. Packer, *God's Plans for You* (Wheaton, IL: Crossway, 2001), 153.

Chapter 10: We Need One Another

1. C. F. Kelley, ed, *The Book of the Poor in Spirit* (London: Longman, Green & Co., 1954), 233.

Chapter 11: You Have a Future

1. Frederick Buechner, *Secrets in the Dark: A Life in Sermons* (New York: HarperCollins, 2007), 237.

ABOUT THE AUTHORS

Patrick and Ruth Schwenk have dedicated their lives to local church ministry, as well as online ministry. They founded the popular blogs FortheFamily.org and TheBetterMom.com, and also the brand-new podcast *Rootlike Faith*. Patrick Schwenk is a pastor of nearly twenty years and the co-author of *For Better or For Kids: A Vow to Love Your Spouse with Kids in the House* and *Faith Forward Family Devotional*. Ruth Schwenk is a well-known blogger and author of *The Better Mom*, *The Better Mom Devotional*, and co-author (with Karen Ehman) of *Pressing Pause* and *Settle My Soul*. Patrick and Ruth have been married for over twenty years and live in Ann Arbor, Michigan, with their four children, two hamsters, and a loyal Labrador retriever.